LOWER HOOK
26 SEP. 94
KINGSTON-ON-THAMES

HOOK
REMEMBERED

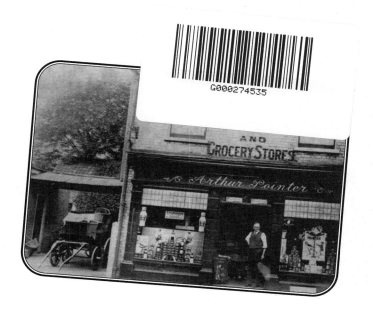

AND GROCERY STORES

Arthur Pointer

*F*OR more than 600 years, this former little village of fruit trees and farms has fostered a thriving community spirit. For older people in Hook, their lasting memory of the hamlet is the flurries of apple and pear blossom which blew off the orchards in spring – or the delightful aroma of newly-baked bread from Pointer's bakery which drifted daily along the Hook Road. The same road was once the home of children's author Enid Blyton and aviation pioneer Harry Hawker. By 1927, the Kingston bypass was open. Developers dangled carrots in front of farmers which were too tempting to resist. By the start of the Second World War, much of Hook's countryside was buried under concrete. What has not been destroyed, however, is the friendly atmosphere and neighbourliness in roads both old and new. Those who care about Hook's future and want to keep it on the map must include its name on their address and not allow the neighbouring names of Chessington, Tolworth and Surbiton to encroach upon its historical identity. In this book, the first photographic volume on old Hook, take a trip down memory lane and beyond. Discover how, although it has changed in so many ways, there are still some rustic houses, cottages and corners which have survived from days of old. And read about some of the characters who have helped to form Hook's special identity over the years.

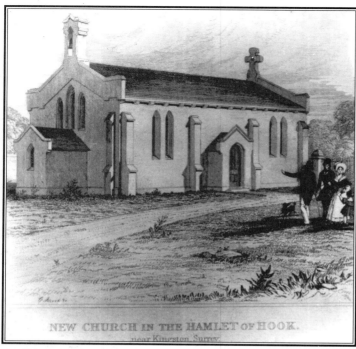

NEW CHURCH IN THE HAMLET OF HOOK.
near Kingston, Surrey.

When Hook's first church was built in 1838, the little hamlet comprised a few farm cottages and a sprinkling of grand houses. There were only 50 inhabited homes in the village. The old church became damp and expensive to run. Towards the end of the 19th century, it wasn't large enough for the expanding community. On St Paul's Day in January 1883, a new church, put up a few yards to the north of the former place of worship, was consecrated. The picture below shows the new St Paul's Church, in about 1905, before the lychgate was erected in memory of James Cundy and Emily and Francis Stephen Clayton in 1914.

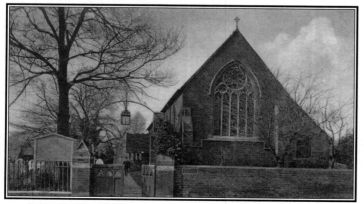

Acknowledgements

Kingston Heritage Centre, Tim Everson and staff; Dennis Stickley and family; Tom and Doris Seymour; Betty Attfield; Albert and Alice Vaughan; Gordon Rex Houle; John Cook; Tina Reynolds; Jeanne Moore; Peter Wallace Butler; Mollie Taylor and neighbours; the late Harold Stevens; Reg Driver; George and Marion Bone; Marjorie Cherry; Phyllis Adams; the late Lilian Coleman; Ted Moore; Sylvia Lewis; Pat Thacker; Pat Donovan; Jack Selby; Gwen Barnes; Margaret Seager; Surrey Local Studies library, Richard Clark and Christine Carpenter; FW Woolworth's; Sainsbury's; Betty Smith, Hook Library staff, Ros Fryer, Gill Whitelock and staff at Surbiton Golf Club; A J Rumble; Jim Mutimer, the late Bill Mutimer and their families; Mrs D Stone, Stan and Mavis Lacey, GPT and Margaret Muggleton; Roger Finch; Phil and Eileen Mepham; Fred and Betty Thompson; Midge Macbeth; Gill Gillingham and the Keene sisters; Susan Vaughan; Norman and Muriel Davison; Eric and Vera Heather; Keith and Joan Easton of Greenhills, Kent; Adriana Van Waarde; Margaret Dare; the late Mrs Nell Ivers; Nigel Davison; June Norton; Brian and John Thompson and other members of the Thompson family; Mrs N Wohanka of Southernhay and the staff of Ransom's (Hook) Plant Hire; representatives of St Paul's Church and the stalwart staff of the marmalade and pickled onion stall; Terry McGinty; Beryl and Bill Boyd; Kathleen, Anne and Lynne Bowyer; various members of the Dudeney family; Margaret Legg; Olive Bell; Ramsay Hughes; Michael Burgess; Roger Finch, the Seager sisters, Nina Fry and staff of St Paul's (Hook) School, including the headmaster, Roger Finch. Mrs E Rook; Mrs D Stone. Paul Adams. Sid Harris and family. Ian and Jenny Currie, E. Parrison, Philip Butler, Nicki Hall, Philip and Mrs Sorley, June Samson, Linda at the Yicken, Dave Swan, Mikey, George Hayward and all the Dorking Pilgrims.

Photograph credits

Royal Borough of Kingston/Kingston Heritage Centre: p1 (Arcade Parade), p18 (Homeware), p26 (Pointer's), p30 (Cecil Lodge and Middleton's outing) p31 (Chessington Court Farm), p36 (Clayton Road bomb), p37, p42 (Gosbury Hill scenes only), p56, p57 (Ace Parade), p58 (library), p59 (Arcade Parade). Mark Davison collection: p1 (Pointer's), p2 (new Hook church), p3, p5, p6, p9, p17 (Arcade Parade, Dudeney and Lineham adverts and signature); p19, p20, p23 (Blyton biographer and Thompson twins); p24 (Child Whispers), p27 (Daily Sketch), p31 (Reg Driver), p39 (Daily Sketch/Mirror), p45 (brick), p52 (Petula Clark), p53 (The Keenes and June Norton), p54 (Hook Roundabout and Southborough Arms), p55, p57 (inscription), p58 (Cohen, R Finch, Mrs Stonard D Wilson), p60 (bus ticket), p62 (65A bus), p64 (all except flood). Betty Smith/Ransoms: p4, p7, p21, p32 (Mutimers), p33 (J Mutimer, plus snowman), p35, p41, p48 (1967 class picture), p58 (house for sale). Surrey Comet: p7, p28 (T. Seymour in retirement), p34, p40 (G Bird), p52, p57 (Francis Stephen Clayton); p63 (Rev. Marsh). The Keenes: p8, p14 (family), p15, p43, p46. Tom Seymour: p12 (Lucky Rover) p27, p28 p29 p38, p43 (1907 school), p45 (school photo). Dennis Stickley and family: p11. Phyllis Adams: p12 (Baileys). Michael Burgess p12 (old White Hart). Dudeney family and Ramsay Hughes: (Mrs Lineham's early life). Keith Easton: The Little Shop. John Thompson and family: p20 (children), p24 (school report), p25 (Enid Blyton and class) Brian Thompson: p22 (sketch), p23 (Thompson brothers). Phil Mepham: p26 (Mepham brothers). Tony Sherwin: p13, p54 (Hook underpass). Hook Library: p14 (Elm Road), p22 (Pelham's Orchard); p27, (war memorial), p32 (Bill Mutimer), p43 (school room poster), p44 (1900 school picture). A J Rumble: p47 (class of 1969); p48 (1969 class). Mr and Mrs Lacey: p49 (school assembly), p50. Mollie Taylor and neighbours: Vallis Way street party. J S Sainsbury plc: p61 (vicars' montage). Eric Heather: p62 (vicars' montage). Clark family: p51 Fred Clark's retirement pictures. Surbiton Golf Club: p30 (fire, Jim Coleman and Dai Rees). Gordon Rex Houle: p33 (POW camp). Rhodrons Club: p40 (house). Stephen Broomhead p64 (flood). D Tippett Wilson: See below.

Bibliography

Special thanks to Marion Bone for her years of hard work unearthing Hook's ancient history resulting in her invaluable reference book, The Story of Hook In Kingston, published by the Parochial Church Council of St Paul, Hook, in 1989. Gillian Watson's unpublished study of Hook in Victorian years, numerous Surrey Comet and Kingston Borough News articles; those from the Comet dating back to the 1880s. St Paul's Church magazines, David Tippett Wilson's collection of scrapbooks and cuttings. Literature held at Hook Library. June Samson. Margaret Bellars' interviews in the 1970s and Marion Bone's miscellaneous items printed since her book was published. Surrey In The Sixties and Surrey in the Seventies. Brian Thompson's unpublished volume of family memories. Jim Mutimer's unpublished volume: Stick and Stones have Broken My Bones. The late Bill Mutimer's unpublished collection of Hook memories. Various documents held at Kingston Heritage Centre. Hook and Southborough Cricket Club, by Geoffrey Latham. Reach For The Sky by Paul Brickhill. Straight From The Kick Off by R Eason.

Editorial assistance by Donald MacPhail and Nigel Davison

Special thanks

Special thanks to David Tippett Wilson of The Yews, Hook Road, for the way he has enthusiastically recorded, on camera and tapes, everyday life in Hook over 30 years. Some of his extensive collection appears on: Pages 10, 23, (W Willcocks), p25 (Mollie Sayer), p48 (Freda Baker), p53 (Eric Blumfield, Bill Cole, Gordon Fischel, Sydney Groves, Bill Mullenger, Midge Macbeth, and Betty Attfield), p59 (Peter Wood), p60 (65 bus) and p63 (Hook scout band).

**Frosted Earth, 77, Rickman Hill, Coulsdon, Surrey CR5 3DT.
Tel 01737 221215**

Copyright October 1997   ISBN 0-9516710-9-X

This book is dedicated to my parents on the occasion of their special wedding anniversary on 27th September 1997.

Printed by Litho Techniques (Kenley), Godstone Road, Whyteleafe, Surrey.

Front cover: Children in Hook Road, near Elm Road, c1905. (Courtesy Phyllis Adams/ David Tippett Wilson). **Back cover:** Hook shopping parade on 23rd July 1962. (Courtesy Kingston Heritage Centre). **Frontispiece:** Hook Road by the Midland Bank, July 1962; Hook Post Office at Pointer's stores c1937 and a post-mark from the same post office in September 1894 (Courtesy Surrey Postal History Group). An earlier "Hook PO", which opened in June 1878, existed in Hook Road by Gladstone Road. It was apparently renamed "Hook Road PO" in 1894 when another sub office opened at Pointer's shop. It is now a 'bookies' at 154 Hook Road.

This is Hook Road at the top of Clayton Road c1915 before the shopping arcades, including Woolworth's, were built. The large building, a former farm stores, became a mop and soaps factory before it was demolished. Budgens supermarket is now on the site.

When it was fields

EVEN as late as the early 1930s, when this photograph was taken, Hook was just a village in the Surrey countryside. These dairy farm fields were soon to be covered under concrete. In 1936 houses were built from the site of 122 Clayton Road in the bottom left-hand corner to the Somerset Avenue estate – on the right – which was yet to be completed.

One finished property in Somerset Avenue can just be seen in the bottom right hand corner, near the marked-out junction with Vallis Way. On the other side of Clayton Road in the picture, Devon Way, Newlands Way and Beverley Close are still to be erected on pasture land.

The Victorian house on the far right is Oaklands, later Yarsley Laboratories, which Herbert Moon, son of Thomas Moon, the Clayton Road dairy farmer, had built.

Hook has been "on the map" since at least the early 13th century, when the southern part of the royal manor of Kingston stretched down in a narrow strip to what is now Fairoak Lane at Malden Rushett.

In her book, *The Story of Hook in Kingston*, Marion Bone chronicles in detail the early history of Hook and examines how the name may have come about. She records how at this time the manors were supervised by sheriffs who collected income for the king from rented land in the manors.

Early in the 12th century, a former Surrey sheriff, Gilbert the Knight, set about founding a monastery in the region. He funded a new order being introduced from the continent – the black-robed Augustinian canons, which King Henry I approved of. The king granted Merton Priory a royal charter in 1121 and it went from strength to strength, boasting several "star" pupils including the martyred saint, Thomas à Becket. The Priory quickly linked up with Kingston Parish Church which had far-flung boundaries reaching to Ditton, Ham and East Molesey.

In 1158, Henry II granted Merton Priory the manor of Ewell. Almost 20 years later, in 1179, "the men of Surbeton" including a John *Hog,* agreed to lease the Merton canons a strip of land at Grapelingeham for 25 years. Cutting out the middle man – the sheriff – in dealing with the king on land issues, seemed the prime motivation for leasing this heel or *hoc*-shaped wedge of agricultural land, even if it involved a few bribes.

Grapelingeham – later The Grapsom – in modern times was the little area of fields and trees a short walk from the rear of Lovelace School, Mansfield Road. It is now mainly buried under the Esher bypass, opened in December 1976.

John Hog – sometimes referred to as John de la *Hoke* – was a key member of the 20-strong "men of Surbeton" with a special interest in land at Hook – or *Hog* or La *Hoke* – in the late 12th and 13th century. The nearby *Hog's*mill river may well be a link. Several families had the name *Hook* after this time.

Hook Rd,
Hook. 1.

The Queen of Hearts tea rooms on the Hook Road next-door-but-one to the Lucky Rover public house provided ices, minerals and light lunches on the lawn for weary cyclists when this picture was taken in the 1920s. Boards outside advertised the Daily Herald newspaper, Mr Bell's hairdressing saloon, free insurance from the Daily Mail and an invitation to purchase St Julien's tobacco. The cafe, also the site in the past of Holly's dairy, for a time supplied dinners to pupils at Hook (St Paul's) School.

CLAYTON HAND LAUNDRY

This old view of Clayton Road is taken from a postcard published in 1912. In the centre can be seen some buildings which were part of Manor Farm which belonged to the Moon family. They kept dairy cows here and were quite advanced in introducing electric milking. Local children delighted in taking a jug up to the farm and collecting milk for their mothers. They were allowed to watch the cows being milked. On the left is Alfred Pearce's laundry and on the right, Manor Farm Cottages, from 1928 home of Jeanne Moore, verger at St Paul's for many years. She was awarded an MBE in the 1990s while still living in the house. (See also page 53).

Milking the cows at Moon's Farm

Clayton Road

Clayton Road between today's Woodgate Avenue and Devon Way, in c1932, showing Moon's dairy farm, right of centre, which supplied milk to Hook and Surbiton. The old Cricketers can also be seen.

CLAYTON Road is one of Hook's oldest lanes. Until 1867, when it was opened as a through route to Woodstock Lane and Claygate, it was sometimes known as Lord King's Lane. The road boasted two beerhouses – the original Cricketers, and The Plough, which stood by the brook close to where Bramham Gardens was built in 1952.

Going up the road, several rows of cottages were erected between the 1880s and the start of the 20th century, including Jeffs Cottages in 1889, Provident Cottages in 1881, Rose Cottages in about 1901 – the year Queen Victoria died – and Clyde Cottage, constructed in 1881.

Some older cottages already existed, including a couple of herdsmen's homes next to the Cricketers. The old pub, replaced in 1938, was a "wooden hut-type structure" with a little footbridge over a ditch outside. In late-Victorian times, displays by dancing bears were sometimes given outside by visiting showmen.

The old Cricketers had a "jug and bottle" bar as well as a saloon and a private bar. In 1871, it was kept by a George Freeman. In 1904, the Cricketers was registered as being a "working class" public house owned by Charrington's. The landlord at that time was James Lee. The pub offered no accommodation or stabling and had only one urinal. It did, however, serve teas in the afternoon. The pub also had an off-licence.

The house on the far right of the picture – in modern times 118 and 120 Clayton Road – was known previously as Manor Farm Cottages. These belonged to Manor Farm opposite, which stood near the spot where Devon Way was built after the Second World War.

Manor Farm was a long building with barns and a cowshed. A path over a stile led through the fields to Claygate. Thomas Moon bought the farm from Thomas Docksey in 1884.

As a young girl in 1928, Jeanne Moore came to live at Manor Farm Cottages when her father James Chappell moved with her mother from a farm in Oxted to work as a dairyman for Sidney Moon, grandson of Thomas Moon. In 1997, the key member of St Paul's Church still lived in the same house. Her mother, Evelyn, who died in 1959, was, like her, a verger at St

Paul's for many years. Jeanne married Harry Moore who, as a young man, worked for his parents' bakery next door to the garage in Hook Road, and was known by some villagers as Boy Moore.

Mrs Moore recalled that when a child, Pearce's Laundry was opposite and the washing used to be hung out to dry. "I can remember them putting the great big sheets through the rollers," she once said. Harry later worked at Hinchley Wood station.

In 1871, Manor Farm Cottages were occupied by agricultural labourers Thomas Webster, Joseph Orpin, James Sapsett and carpenter Joseph Hart.

Living next door, in another large house, Rosebank, 100 yards down the road on the same side, was a laundress, Elizabeth Knight. This house, too, survived up to the 21st century. The cottages dotted around this part of the farming village were collectively known as Lower Hook, and included a row called The Laurels which were demolished in the 1960s to build Linda Court.

A number of farm hands working for Mr Moon on his 188 acres also lived in humble dwellings at Lower Hook.

An advertisement in the Surrey Comet in April 1887, placed by Thomas Moon of Manor Farm, Clayton Road, who had taken on premises in Surbiton to supply milk from his growing herd of shorthorn and Alderney cows at Hook.

[CIRCULAR]

MANOR FARM DAIRY,

21, VICTORIA ROAD,

SURBITON, April, 1887.

SIR OR MADAM,—

A short time ago, I announced my intention of delivering Milk direct from my Farm. Since that time I have received so much support that I find it necessary, in order to meet the increased demand, to take the above premises, which were OPENED on APRIL 18th, 1887, as a FIRST-CLASS DAIRY, for the Sale of Milk and other Dairy Produce from my Farm. The Cows are well bred, Shorthorns and choice Alderneys, and they may be seen at any time grazing on the extensive meadows of the Farm, which is within one and a-half miles of the Dairy.

The close proximity of the Farm, with its perfect sanitary and other arrangements, will enable me to supply an article quite equal in FRESHNESS and PURITY to any milk produced by Alderney Cows at Gentlemen's own places.

I remain, Sir or Madam,

Your obedient Servant,

THOMAS H. MOON.

Two schoolgirl friends enjoy the open countryside at Clayton Road c1932 before the Somerset Avenue "Hooklands" estate is completed. Mrs Evelyn Chappell, later a verger at St Paul's Church for many years, is seen with daughter, Jeanne, right, and pal, Marjorie Keene, born at the Laurels, Clayton Road, in 1923. The picture was taken behind Jeanne's home.

Life at the Laurels

LONG before Linda Court was built in 1960 at Clayton Road, there stood a row of mid-Victorian homes called the Laurels which were once a hive of activity.

Running a laundry business at the cottages around the time of the First World War and for many years after were Mary and Ernest Pike.

The Laurels, bought originally by Mr Pike for £100, also offered much-needed affordable accommodation for young Hook couples struggling to make ends meet. Newlyweds often lived in two rooms of the villas.

The laundry occupied two rooms on one side of the house. The Pikes' grand-daughter, Marjorie Keene, who was born at the Laurels in 1923, recalled in later life: "There was a great big wood-burning copper boiler. All on one side were big wooden tubs and on the floors were duckboards on which they stood and scrubbed the washing. There was also a coke boiler stove in the drying room and big wooden driers all around that looked like giant clotheshorses."

Marjorie, whose married name was Dunford, also recalled a small band of employees, the most memorable of whom was Mrs Marsh, who lived in the now-vanished cottages opposite Shadbolts' sweet shop in Clayton Road.

"She had a cap, smoked a pipe and had no teeth."

Mrs Marsh had a daughter, Nellie, who worked at the rival Clayton Laundry, run originally by Alfred Pearce and his family next door to the Cricketers pub.

Marjorie's grandmother used to serve the families in the large Victorian houses along the Brighton Road in Surbiton and deliver the laundered linen and garments on a handcart she pushed through the streets of Hook and Southborough.

Ernest Pike, of The Laurels, used to terrify his grandchildren who were scared to sit next to him at the meal table. But one day, he burst out laughing when his great-grandson, John, told him: "Haven't you got a big nose?" He agreed. And he always wore "that" belt otherwise "I might get a chill in me 'stommick'."

Clayton Rd.
HOOK.

The Plough alehouse in Clayton Road – nearest building on the right – ceased trading as a public house in 1898 when it was sold by Charrington's brewers. Although for a time it is said to have sold confectionery after its days as a beerhouse, it was pulled down some years after this photograph was taken in about 1920. The now-vanished houses over the road, by the brook, often flooded.

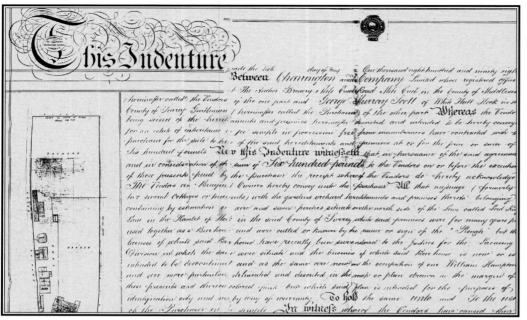

The Plough beerhouse, "Lord King's Lane" (Clayton Road) was sold in 1898.

Peppermint King of Clayton Road

THE Plough beerhouse in "Lord King's Lane" (Clayton Road, between today's piped-in brook and Bramham Gardens) was sold by Charrington's brewery to George Murray Scott of Whitehall, Hook, on 6th May 1898 for £600, after which it was no longer a pub. Whitehall stood where Whitehall Crescent was built in 1939.

In its latter years, the alehouse, which could not sell spirits, was kept by licencee Henry Moore, whose son, Arthur, was known as the Peppermint King because all he drank were peppermint cordials. Arthur's grandson, Ted Moore, aged 89 in October 1997, lived for many years in Hemsby Road, Chessington. Another grandson, Harold, who lived in retirement at Leatherhead Road, recalled that his mother, Agnes, was a barmaid at The Plough, Surbiton, when she met Henry Moore.

The Plough beerhouse had grounds of "one acre and seven perches" stretching back 382ft in which were an orchard, cowhouse, pond, piggery, stable, chaff and chicken sheds and a manure heap. The frontage was 100ft long. Henry became a pig farmer at Gosbury Hill but lost his herd to swine fever.

The building survived as a pair of cottages into the 20th century and was home for years to the Tidy family who kept beautiful rose gardens and gave bunches of flowers to local children. Some say confectionery was sold there for a time.

Whitehall, the large mansion and stables over the road, was sold in 1938 for redevelopment. A small row of semi-detached houses stands where the Plough once served refreshments. A Labour councillor, Peter Alexander, and his family lived for more than four decades in 34 Clayton Road, where the beerhouse stood. Living opposite in the 1980s was Debbie McGee who married magician Paul Daniels. The TV star was sometimes seen parking his car nearby while visiting Debbie, who lived with her parents at the house and earlier attended Tolworth Girls School.

Whitehall had a drawing room, dining room, breakfast room, study, an occasional room and morning room on the ground floor and six main bedrooms on the first floor. Three bedrooms were in a separate wing for the servants. The stables had three loose boxes and the gardens contained three glasshouses.

Whitehall

WHITEHALL was a late Georgian nine-bedroom mansion with greenhouses and stables.

In 1839 it was home for two years to Reverend John McCammon Trew, first full-time minister at Hook Church.

Born in Ireland in about 1794, he lived at Whitehall with his wife, Ann, three sons, four daughters and five servants. After two years, he left to become an archdeacon in the Bahamas.

In 1871, it was home to East India merchant Robert Scurfield.

George Murray Scott and family were the occupants of Whitehall in the first part of the 20th century. Among his staff was a coachman, Mr Attwill, whose daughter, Lilian Coleman (nee Attwill) lived most of her life in Clayton Road, firstly at no. 62 in one of the Victorian cottages, and in married life at 66, with husband, Jim, a professional golfer for 50 years at Surbiton Golf Club.

Mr Attwill, who lost a son in the First World War, also looked after the Scotts' horses. The house's domestic offices included a scullery, larder, maids' sitting room, butler's pantry and garden lobby. George Murray Scott died in 1927.

The Stickley farmers

WITHOUT the Stickleys, Hook could only have been something like a farm without a farmer. The Stickley family's link with the village goes back to the late 1850s when three brothers arrived from Kent and soon established themselves as enterprising farmers and council sub-contractors in Hook Road.

Originally, the family came from Bere Regis, Dorset. James Stickley, born 1828, had nine children by his first marriage, to Jane Davis. Sons James Melmoth, born 1840, John James, (1832), and Matthew, (1847) came from Kent to Hook, seeking work.

James Stickley's great-great-great-grandson, Dennis Stickley, living in 1997 at Leatherhead Road, Malden Rushett, was one of seven brothers and sisters brought up next door to the Lucky Rover at Woodstock, 314 Hook Road, later the UCS car accessories supplies and then a video repair shop In 1997, Roy, June and Hazel were living at Lancing, Sussex, while Philip lived in Ashcroft Road, Hook.

When they were children, Woodstock had an acre of orchards at the back with large pear trees. The children used to step over a plank leading from the orchard to the gardens of neighbouring Cecil Lodge.

The Stickleys kept Haycroft Farm. The farmhouse stood almost where the Southborough Arms was built and came down when the Kingston bypass was constructed. The Stickleys ran a hugely successful depot opposite Haycroft Road providing horse-drawn refuse collection and road building services and then a coal delivery business.

The Stickleys' prize-winning corn ricks opposite the North Star before the Parish Hall was built in 1926. In the pub's forecourt is an open-topped bus waiting to return to Kingston and Ealing. This farmland later became a children's playing field with swings, a slide and roundabout.

Charles Edward Stickley – great-grandfather of Dennis – outside Haycroft Farm in about 1900. It was demolished when the Kingston bypass was built.

John James Stickley, centre, with farmhand Yates and head ploughman Ike Wiltshire, with Stickley's prize-winning horses pictured around 1900. The photograph was taken opposite Haycroft Road, Hook, after a May Day competition held at the Victoria Recreation Ground, Surbiton. One of the prizes was for the best-conditioned horse; the other for best-decorated horse.

The old White Hart

THE old White Hart (right) was a humble roadside public house which was pulled down in the 1930s and rebuilt with a new, much larger building set back from the road and thriving in modern times. According to Surrey licencing records, in 1904 the landlord was a Henry Stripp, the pub had no sleeping accommodation, could offer stabling for four horses, had just one urinal and served no refreshments other than alcohol.

Its history goes back to the 1700s and it is believed an even earlier building may have stood on the site. It was never a coaching inn.

In the 1940s and 1950s its forecourt served as a bus terminus for the 65 double-decker buses to and from Ealing and Kingston, before the service was extended to Chessington and Leatherhead on a regular basis.

A life-long Hook resident, Reg Driver, who, in 1997, was living in retirement at Shere Close, enjoyed a regular pint of beer in the hostelry from 1934 – when he was 16 – to well into the 1990s. And he was still able to cycle up to 60 miles a day at the age of 78.

In the 18th century, Hook's village business was often conducted at a type of parish council known as a vestry. Some of these meetings were held at the White Hart around the 1760s.

The old White Hart before demolition in the 1930s. The old house in the background on the left is Whitehall. In the late 19th century, an inquest was held in the White Hart after a fatal accident outside the Rhodrons.

The Lucky Rover darts club in 1928. Lifelong Hook resident Tom Seymour is pictured by the front door as a 19-year-old. He's the dapper one, sporting a bow tie and Trilby hat.

Lucky Rover's adventures

DRINKING was a favourite pastime of Hook's menfolk. On summer outings to the sea, the Lucky Rover regulars used to down up to five pints before boarding a motor coach to the coast and on reaching Leatherhead, deemed it necessary for a top-up. On arrival at the seafront, they made a beeline for the nearest bar and then boarded a steamer, enjoying further liquid refreshments.

The journey home was a long and hot one, requiring comfort stops at places such as Cobham's inns. And it was vital to get back before last orders at the Lucky.

In late Victorian times, Hook's seven public houses served a 'drinking' population of just 150 people. These little intimate pubs were places to go, exchange gossip and maybe talk about subjects such as the decline of agriculture. They also served as shops. The Lucky in 1851 sold groceries and meat; the Southborough Arms, farm produce.

Lewis Bailey and his wife were landlords of The Lucky Rover in Edwardian times.

Hook Road as it was in about 1912, looking south from the top of the Clayton Road junction. On the left is Vane Cottage, built in 1669, three years after the Great Fire of London. It was still standing as the millennium approached. The old White Hart is on the right.

Childhood days in Elm Road

Elm Road, Hook, Surbiton

Elm Road used to be the main route from Hook to Ewell and Epsom before the building of Bridge Road. In Victorian times, it was called Ewell Road. Children used to call out to returning Epsom racegoers: "Throw out your mouldy coppers!". This picture is dated 1912.

A well-known Hook family over the years have been the Keenes. This picture, taken in about 1912, shows Lizzie Keene in the garden of Myrtle Cottages, - now 53 Elm Road - with five of her nine children. At the top is Ivy, and on the right, Holly. On the left is Marjorie, and on her mother's lap is Rene. At the front is Ted. They all went to Hook School.

ELM Road was home to several characters in bygone times. Apart from the anti-motor car campaigner, Georgie Bird, of The Rhodrons, there were several others in the first part of the 20th century.

Aggie Carpenter of Orchard Place was "a card". She made daily trips to the Lucky Rover and returned with a jug of beer.

Mrs Ingram, of Myrtle Cottages, had a wooden leg and used to travel by bus, always causing chaos because it took so long for her to swing the artificial limb on board.

George Busk always went around with a bowler hat and the children in the road believed he must have slept in it.

A forge was run by Bill Gee who had a motorbike and sidecar. He sometimes delighted the neighbours' children by taking them for rides in it. He used to make horseshoes for the local farmers such as the Moons.

There was a big chestnut tree outside the forge in the centre of the yard which survived into modern times.

A family snapshot taken in the garden of Myrtle Cottages, Elm Road in about 1927. At the back are Charlie Keene and Lizzie Keene. Sitting behind young Gwen Keene is "Grandpa Larkin".

Hook's only midwife, Polly Hillier, lived at Myrtle Cottages, now 47 Elm Road, opposite the forge in the '20s.

Holly and Ivy (right and left) were two of the nine children of Lizzie and Harry Keene, of 53 Elm Road, Hook. Holly, born in 1903, moved to Hampton and married a carpenter, Bill, who worked at Shepperton Studios. Ivy married a Kent sailor.

The life of Mrs Lineham

FEW of Hook's older residents can forget the Victorian-style postmistress and shopkeeper, Margaret Lineham. With her grey hair worn in a bun, her sombre dress sense and strict, no-nonsense attitude, she was a figure who perpetuated the days of a bygone era.

Mrs Lineham opened up "Hook, Surbiton Post Office" in Arcade Parade, close to JS Wood's the butcher's shortly after the Second World War. The post office had previously been across the road at Pointer's general stores, and in the late 1930s, Mrs Lineham is said to have worked there for a time, gaining what would prove to be valuable experience for future years.

Born on January 3rd 1889, Maggie, as she was known, was one of nine children of George Dudeney, a master grocer and remarkable businessman in Bedford. Her mother was George's first cousin, Jane.

The Dudeney family were exceedingly bright, often temperamental, and sometimes lacked a sense of humour, according to descendants.

George Dudeney was born at Plumpton, Sussex, in 1851. His father, Samuel, was a farmer and a member of a Huguenot family which settled in the 16th century. His uncle, John Dudeney, born 1782, was a Sussex worthy: a self-educated shepherd boy who studied maths and Hebrew from books he kept in a hole in the chalk downs and went on to become a noted mathematician and schoolmaster. His bust is in Lewes Museum.

Maggie's father left school at eight years old but by diligent study became a well-read man. At the age of 12 he went to Brighton for business training and here he opened his first grocery shop in 1874 at the age of 23.

One of Maggie's brothers, Leonard, became a Fleet Street journalist. Her brother Walter became mayor of Brighton in 1954, and another, Albert, Mayor of Bedford. Yet another brother, Harold, was selected to be Mayor of Worthing but refrained owing to his wife's objections.

As for Maggie, after leaving Bedford High School she worked at the various branches of her father's master grocer's stores around Bedford. The stores were thriving concerns and included tea rooms, a bakery, restaurants and even a dance hall, "The Dudj". Shopkeeping was in her blood.

Maggie's family became wealthy and bought a large house, Brooklands, in Newport Pagnell in 1920. It was here

Mrs Lineham in 1952.

In the Great War, Maggie, left, packed loaves for prisoners of war in Germany at the family's Dudeney and Johnston bakery in Bedford with friend and sister-in-law, Gertrude Dudeney.

that she met her future husband, widower Thomas Lineham, who ran a grocery stores and outfitter's in the town. An earlier boyfriend is said to have died in the First World War. In the war, Maggie "for a time drove ambulances".

She married Thomas in September 1925 at the parish church in the delightful Buckinghamshire village of Emberton near Newport Pagnell where they set up home. They helped to raise a young girl, Joan Lineham, who was Thomas's grand-daughter. Thomas Lineham was many years older than Maggie and must have appreciated her help in his shop. He is remembered by Maggie's niece, Ramsay Hughes, as a "very charming and kind man." It was a rather unusual marriage and was to last only 11 years. In January 1937, Thomas died. It

was the second blow for Mrs Lineham. Five years earlier her 80-year-old father had died.

Around this time, Mrs Lineham moved to Surrey to be near her spinster sister, Dora, a respected Middlesex nurse, and another sister, May. Maggie's widowed mother, Jane, was now living in Carshalton Beeches where she died, deaf and blind, in March 1938 and where Maggie's sister, Dora, died just two months later.

In the early years of the last war, Mrs Lineham owned a wool shop, Broderies, in Brighton Road, Surbiton. However, her career took a side step when she went to help run Kingston Hill Post Office, in Park Road, owing to the shortage of menfolk. An opportunity then arose to take on

Margaret Lineham with her grocer husband, Thomas Lineham, and his grand-daughter who they helped to bring up in the years before Mrs Lineham came to Hook.

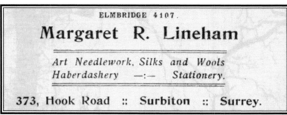

Mrs Lineham was 72 when this 'ad' appeared in Hook church magazine in March 1961.

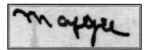

Left: Mrs Lineham sitting on her mother's lap at the age of three in 1892. Her father by now was a highly successful master grocer in Bedford. It was at his various branches of the Dudeney and Johnston chain that Maggie gained the skills to run her shop at Hook during the fifties and early sixties. Her brother Albert, far right, is wearing a black armband after the death of baby brother, John.

Thomas Lineham's stores, Newport Pagnell, 1925.

Hook, Surbiton post office c1948 run by Mrs Lineham.

her own post office in Hook. This occurred when Arthur Pointer decided to concentrate on the bakery and grocery side of his Hook Road shop. Mrs Lineham sold wools, haberdashery, toys and stationery from 373 Hook Road, (in later years a washeteria). Any child who misbehaved was reprimanded. Marjorie Cherry, who worked at the wool shop with her in Surbiton was asked to assist at Hook. "She knew I knew her funny ways," said Marjorie in later life. "She was like a sergeant major in the forces. She was very strict."

Another setback occurred in May 1955 when a new Crown PO opened in Elm Road, 100 yards from her store. Her sub office shut but the toys and wool shop continued until 1965, with Mrs Lineham living in a flat above. Inside her home were many boxes of withdrawn or surplus stock. She slept only in an armchair, with a little gas stove beside her for making tea. PC Sid Harris and his wife, Iris, often called to make sure she was well. Mrs Lineham befriended Miss Olive Bell, supervisor at the new PO. The two went on outings to places such as Leicester Square Odeon and to see Margaret's brother Walter in Brighton. Mrs Lineham died on 2nd January 1976 in Richmond after being hospitalised.

A 1925 advertisement for Maggie's father's shop which by now was being run by her brothers Albert and Percy.

The Little Shop

The Little shop in about 1960.

FOR at least 70 years, families relied on the Little Shop at Jeffs Cottages, Clayton Road, for sweets, ice cream and the odd items of groceries they had forgotten to purchase elsewhere.

The store was run for decades by the Shadbolts. Mr Shadbolt was also a hairdresser and he enjoyed a drink. Local children were worried should his hand slip while holding the cut-throat razor.

At the rear of the higgledy piggledy shop, where "you could buy anything" was a parrot in a cage. The Aladdin's cave of a shop even had a medicine cabinet almost hanging off the wall in the Shadbolts' days.

In the 1950s, George and Elsie Goodard took over. He was a football player of note.

Keith and Joan Easton arrived in 1958, after Joan's father-in-law, Thomas Gull, bought the freehold. They left in the mid 1970s. The new owners had the shop for only a year before it sadly shut for good.

The Eastons moved to Herne Bay in 1989.

Worker found mice in bag

The Homeware

ORIGINALLY built as a corn and fruit store when Hook was a small farming village, the "Homeware" building attempted to keep up with modern development by becoming a factory before the Second World War.

Homeware Co (Hook) Ltd, opened c1924, was run in the 1930s by three brothers, Bill, Roland and Jimmy Long. Its workforce of between 12 and 20 produced mops, soaps and polishes, together with other domestic kitchen goods.

One employee in the late 1930s was Adriana "Mina" Van-Waarde, born in Elm Road in 1917.

She started work at the factory in 1935 and her job was chiefly to make mops by sewing the strands together.

"There was a big door at the front and a side entrance," Miss Van-Waarde recalled many years later. "The staff went in through the side door and climbed up the stairs into this big room where we sat with these machines, making the mops. We all sat along these long benches and there were two women supervisors to keep an eye on us."

She said that on one occasion she put her hand into a sack to remove some material and, to her horror, discovered there were mice in it.

People in Hook felt grateful to have a factory amid the little community which offered employment. One villager reflected: "It was quite something."

Another senior citizen remembered that some people called the Homeware the "O-Cedar Mop Co" apparently after the name of the product printed on tins in which the mop heads were stored.

Elderly residents have had stories passed

The Homeware Co (Hook) Ltd factory which stood on the Hook Road making mops and polishes. It was formerly a fruit stores.

down that the building was erected for the Moons at Manor Farm, Clayton Road, who had vast acres of land on the west side of Hook Road before the Somerset Avenue estate was built and further agricultural land opposite the White Hart where acres of potatoes grew. Farm and garden produce including peaches, nectarines, green figs and quinces were sold from this fruit and vegetable store.

After its demolition in the sixties, the site was redeveloped as a supermarket in the early seventies for Bishops whose small grocery shop in the neighbouring parade – next to Matthew's the butchers – had proved too small to cope with the expanding population of the community.

After the devastating fire at Bishops in 1984, the supermarket reopened as Budgens and remained under this name at the approach of the millennium.

The Homeware stood between Woolworth's and Pointer's stores. In its last days, it was surrounded by a tall fence which curious schoolboys used to peer over. At the rear was scrubland leading to the gardens of numbers 2, 4 and 6, Bramham Gardens. This wasteland, once the site of a pond, proved a popular playground for children from the local area.

In Marion Bone's book, *The Story of Hook in Kingston*, she states the belief that the building was constructed as a granary for a member of George Murray Scott, of Whitehall, Hook, for a member of his family – probably HY Scott, who worked as a miller and forage contractor.

Hook Post Office and Pointer's bakery and general stores (later the National Westminster Bank) in about 1937. Two doors up from Pointer's is a newsagent's and sweetshop, then Woodstock (no.314 Hook Road) where the Stickley family were raised.

1920s schooldays with Enid Blyton

ENID Blyton wrote her first book in Hook after being inspired by the little group of children she taught in a private school in Hook Road. The creativity she gained from the youngsters during her four years at Southernhay, 207 Hook Road, from 1920 to 1924 led her to become the world's most prolific children's writer with 600 books to her name.

Hook Road was sprinkled with chippings and sand but was not metalled outside Southernhay in the early 1920s. The distant poplars on the right mark the house.

Enid Blyton, took up a residency as a governess and teacher at Southernhay with the aim of educating the four sons of Horace and Gertrude Thompson who moved into the early 19th-century mansion in May 1911.

On 17th January 1913, Horace, a chartered surveyor, and his wife celebrated after the birth of their first son, Brian. The announcement of his birth was published on the front page of the *Times*.

In a vivid self-penned memoire of his life, newspaperman Brian Thompson looked back in retirement on those happy years.

He wrote that Southernhay was then a three-storey house built around 1814 and in the front garden were two magnificent poplar trees which flanked the wooden entrance gate. The circular driveway enclosed a clump of large rhododendrons.

The house stood 100 feet back from the road and the trees muffled the sound of an occasional passing motor car.

' The garden must have been about a couple of acres, running at the back and on the south side, with a grass tennis court, greenhouse, summer house, pond for ducks, hen house, rabbit hutch and some fine mature trees, particularly a chestnut and a weeping elm upon which a swing was fixed.

The south boundary was a high wooden fence with large steps attached so that we could – and did – climb over into what we called Stickley's field. It was a small, little-used field, belonging to the Stickley farmer whose farm buildings (*Haycroft*) were immediately beyond.

On the north and east side of Southernhay was the house and very large garden of Brocket, where lived Mr Walter Willcocks, his spinster daughter, Winnie, and her friend, Ethel Catley. We called the ladies 'auntie' but Mr Willcocks was never 'uncle' – oh dear, no. He was a short, stocky man, always dressed immaculately in black, who worked in the City and was driven there daily in a chauffeured car. He seemed to demand, and certainly got, unfailing respect.

In the kitchen at Brocket (*now Cooper House*) with which my three brothers and I were more familiar, was a cook called Gosden and two maids. Many a freshly-baked cake did we have from Gosden.

At the top of the garden were steps up into the higher ground of Brocket garden. No gate. We just came and went as we pleased, but always treated the Willcocks' ground with much the same awe that we held for Mr Willcocks himself. No games, no noise. Mostly would we brandish butterfly nets, for they had a large buddleia by the kitchen door which always seemed to be festooned with tortoiseshell, peacock and red admiral butterflies.

Beyond the Brocket garden were fields as far as one could see. Occasionally we would take

John Thompson pictured at Southernhay, Hook Road, in 1919 at the age of four.

John's brother, Peter, at four.

Hook Road in the early 1930s. The tall trees on the left screen Brocket and Southernhay. The latter was home of Enid Blyton from 1920 to 1924. King Edward's Drive and the Hook recreation ground are on the right.

a picnic tea into the nearest of these fields.

I took a walk down Hook Road towards the end of 1987. The two poplar trees and the front gardens of Southernhay and Brocket had been acquired *(in 1963)* for the construction of a dual carriageway, and the houses looked so different I did not recognise them at all. Southernhay, almost opposite Hook recreation ground, was a doctors' surgery and was now no. 207 Hook Road. It was covered in a creeper. Brocket House was the headquarters of the General and Municipal Boilermakers' Union. It was only some years later that I was informed these were the same two buildings as in my childhood.

Behind Brocket and Southernhay were countless houses and even a railway, one running to Chessington. The recreation ground was still there, but further down on that side, which had been common land strewn with gorse bushes *(Kelvin Grove area)* were substantial houses and more houses.

The road leading to Stickley's farm was now Hunters Road, a typical suburban road with houses on both sides.

The changed scene interested rather than depressed me. After all it was 63 years since I left and just 50 since I had been back. The visit prompted me to put my memories on paper.

I was one of four boys: David, born in February 1911; myself in 1913, and twins John and Peter in June 1915. Mother kept a progress book in which she recorded birth statistics, early weights, vaccinations, illnesses, "funny sayings", early schooling, holidays, religious progress and the like. Into it she pasted our early scribbling and painting attempts. She kept it meticulously for David and myself, but obviously found it a bit of a chore when the babies came along.

According to this record book, I was born on 17th January 1913 at 9.30am, one month premature and weighing seven and a half pounds. I lost nearly a pound in the first two days and then made uninterrupted progress.

Sheep were kept in Pelham's orchard, now the Coniston Way and Willcocks Close area. The fruit orchards were part of the Stickley family's vast farm covering much of the land east of Hook Road. Southernhay was previously known as Pelham House. Willcocks Close was named after Walter Willcocks.

My hair was blond and curly. When I had my first haircut at two years and five months, a blond curl was put in an envelope and survived well into my retirement years.

My first prayer, said on mother's knee, was: "Thank you for the chickens. Thank you for making Mother and dear Daddy. Thank you for all the clothes we have on and don't let the soldiers get hurt!" Note my priorities!

That reference to the soldiers was therefore in March 1915, the eighth month of the Great War, which was to last for four years. I have few recollections of those war years. I can remember Mother, clad in a white overall, standing by the kitchen range baking bread. There was no rationing but food was short.

By mid 1915, there were four babies to feed, all under four and a half years old. Mother told me in later years that she had to dismiss a parlour maid – because she ate too much.

In the bedroom in which David and I slept, there was a bay and this could be curtained off. I recall seeing my father putting his puttees on one evening as he donned his khaki uniform. He was a chartered surveyor by profession, working for a firm entitled Nightingale, Page and Bennett, with offices just below Surbiton station. He was turned down for active service on health grounds but volunteered for munition manufacturing at Acton by day and the equivalent of Home Guard duty by night.

I also have faint recollections of being lifted from my bed by mother during the night and taken down the steep, dark steps into the basement because a German zeppelin was in the vicinity. My clearest memory is of the declaration of an Armistice at the 11th hour of the 11th day of the 11th month – 11th November 1918.

David and I went to school as usual that day to St Bernard's, about a mile down the road to

Surbiton. In mid-morning, the head mistress told us all that there would be no more lessons because the war was over and we were all too joyful to do any work.

Everyone would go home except those whose names she would mention. Ours were among them. We were to wait to be picked up. We waited by the gate and in due course saw our mother walking down the Upper Brighton Road toward us. She told us she was taking us up to London by train from Surbiton to celebrate. At Trafalgar Square, there was a huge crowd making merry. Clearly Mother feared for our safety and two army officers in uniform came to her aid. They lifted us onto their shoulders

Enid Blyton's sketch of Brian at the seaside in September 1920.

22

and stood for a time in a shop doorway.

Before long it was deemed better that Mother returned home with us, so we all retreated to the Underground station once more, where David and I were handed back into parental control.

Most days at the junction outside St Bernard's School (*now the A243 Upper Brighton Road*) was a crossing sweeper, whose job was to direct traffic and sweep up horse droppings. He had lost a leg in the war and sported a wooden one. My father and others used to hand him a Christmas box each year.

There was very little traffic on the roads those days and we often walked the mile home to Southernhay. We often walked in the roadway, for if a car were to come, we would hear it a long way off and it would be travelling slowly. I think my only fear was of Russian soldiers with snow on their boots! A silly story which we must have heard people tell in jest, but I recall many a time turning round a little frightened when we heard footsteps of someone catching up on us!

In 1919, the last of a succession of nurses left, and according to the family progress book, Mother gave a sigh of relief. Life had centred mainly around the nursery. We had all our meals there, except Sunday tea, which we had with our parents in the drawing room. Sunday tea was a great event, chiefly because it included one cake – the only one of the week – and then, only after a reasonable intake of bread and butter.

I remember little about these nurses apart from their peculiarities. Nurse Domesday was inclined to dribble while speaking. Nurse Tanner, plump and caring, found a large death's head hawk moth after she left and sent it to us in a matchbox with a pin through its head but still alive.

Discipline was strict but loving. Perhaps there were occasions when I had reservations about the loving part, such as when I refused my rice pudding and had to sit at the table with the offending concoction in front of me well into the afternoon until both of us were stiff and cold and it was removed ungraciously.

When we no longer had nurses, we had all our meals in the dining room with our parents. Meal times were scrupulously observed. For breakfast, the gong was sounded at 7.55. At eight o'clock sharp, the door was locked against anyone not yet down and properly dressed and there was no compromise – no breakfast.

Conversation at meal times was orderly and nicely balanced between the adult and childish interests. Looking back, I think the most common topic was David Lloyd George. He was Liberal Prime Minister from 1916 to 1922 and my parents were devout Liberals. Lloyd George often used to wear a slouch hat and we were very fond of boiled apple puddings which in some way resembled headgear. "Hooray! Lloyd George's hat" we used to cry as the maid placed the pudding on the

The 'Famous Three' Thompsons: from left to right: Brian with twins John and Peter at Southernhay, (207 Hook Road) in about 1923, three years into Enid Blyton's residency as their governess.

table. I don't think my parents' admiration for Lloyd George ever waned.

Towards the end of 1919, Mother was taken ill and could no longer look after four lively boys. So, for the time being, David was sent to live at Runnymede, Cobham, the home of family friend Leonard Bentall, of Bentall's store, and I was sent to Hunstanton, Norfolk, to stay with an aunt and uncle.

When Mother's health improved the following year, we were all reunited back at Southernhay. Those two years after the end of the

The Thompsons' neighbour, Walter Willcocks, of Brocket, Hook Road, was a great benefactor to Hook.

war are very vivid to me, even 60 years later. I can remember the telephone number of Southernhay (Kingston 554) although I sometimes have difficulty now in remembering my current one!

Dad was still working with Nightingale, Page and Bennett. A five-and-a-half day week, too, for this was the norm. He would leave home at midday on a Saturday and when he returned there would be David and myself at the window looking out for him, for the first thing he would do on coming inside was to put his right hand in his pocket and bring out our weekly pocket money – 1d (or 0.4p) each.

How we looked forward to that! After lunch, we were allowed to go up the road to the little group of shops (*in Hook Road*

Peter and John Thompson back at Southernhay with Enid Blyton's biographer Barbara Stoney in December 1992.

just past the Ace) and spend it. Into Seymour's newsagents we would go, having discussed our purchases on the way, and either buy a pennyworth of 'hundreds and thousands' each or pool our vast resources and buy a twopenny copy of The Rainbow, to read all about Mrs Bruin, the Bruin Boys and especially Tiger Tim.

Our only other reading matter was delivered: Arthur Mee's Children's Newspaper, which was bought for us, for reasons not difficult to guess.

David and I were very close. We played together happily and we slept in the same room. At one time, after going to bed, we decided to count up to a million. We would take it in turns, one counting aloud and the other mentally ticking off the hundreds and thousands and keeping the running total. The only difficulty was that the teller sometimes fell asleep

first, unobserved, which resulted in something of an argument the next night over the total he had reached.

I have no idea how far we got before calling the whole thing off – certainly not a million.

On a summer evening we could peep out between the curtains and see a tennis party in progress on the grass court below, or from another window we could just see, at an angle, about 11 o'clock, Dad playing cricket for Hook Cricket Club.

On Sundays we attended Kingston Congregational Church Sunday school where our parents were teachers.

Most Sunday afternoons we would take the bus with Dad to places such as Oxshott Woods, Chessington or Leatherhead.

Our first family transport was a motorbike with a sidecar. Then came a secondhand 1913 Argyle. It was an open car with running boards on each side

CHILD WHISPERS
By ENID BLYTON

Child Whispers was Enid Blyton's first published book. She wrote it in her study at Southernhay, Hook, in 1922.

and a hood which folded back so it could be strapped down. If it rained, we would stop the car, jump out and pull the hood over.

We would then take out some side pieces with perspex-type windows and fasten them along each side.

The lamps were on brackets and were carbide-filled and lit with a match. Not infrequently, one or both would blow out and need to be re-lit. I recall an occasion in Kingston when the fog was so thick that Dad made us walk in front of the car, David and myself each taking a lamp off its bracket and holding it in front of the car to guide Dad on

The Hook Road lamplighter

THE Thompson boys took a great interest in tradesmen as well as the lamplighter and the postman. The postman came with three deliveries a day – at about 8am, midday and 4.30pm. It was not unusual to receive mail by the evening delivery which had been posted locally that same morning, Brian recalled.

"The lamplighter in Hook Road carried a long pole with a hook on the end. The street lights were gas and each had a switch centrally fixed with a ring at each end. At sundown and dawn, the lamplighter would insert the hook at the end of his pole into the appropriate end of the switch and so light the lamp from the pilot light."

A school report from Enid, 1922

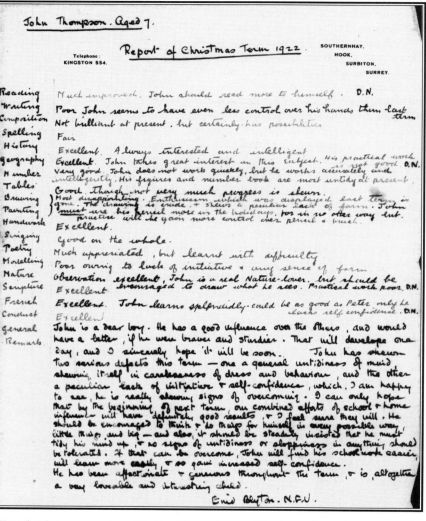

Enid Blyton wrote of John Thompson: "He is a dear boy; a real nature lover but needs to be sturdier and braver".

his way.

The milkman called daily, but not with bottles. On his cart would be large churns of milk and he would ladle it out into our own jugs left on the doorstep.

The baker also made a daily call and the grocer and greengrocer two calls – one to take an order and the second to bring the goods requested. Our parents never considered making their own purchases and carrying them home. '

Tales of tadpoles, fairies and butterflies

Nature lessons with Auntie Enid

ENID Blyton was brought to Southernhay by the Thompson family because Mrs Thompson's health was suffering and two of the sons were back from boarding school or long stays with relatives. She needed someone to help out with their education.

David was nine, Brian seven, and Peter and John just five when she arrived in 1920. David was due to go to Mill Hill School and they did not think he would pass the entrance exams. Extra lessons were required.

Horace Thompson's cousin, Mabel Attenborough, in Beckenham, recommended her best friend, Enid Blyton, as being suitable to help out.

The Froebel-trained teacher took up residence in a rear upper room at Southernhay and was adored by the Thompson boys who were soon joined by neighbours' children for lessons.

They went out in the lanes catching butterflies, walked through the meadows at Gosbury Hill, and caught tiddlers in a stream near Moor Lane. And they let off a small hot air balloon from Hook recreation ground with an address tag which was eventually returned from Belgium after which the young charges studied geography maps showing the route it flew.

In 1921, Enid's first work was published in Cassells Magazine.

The following year, her first book, Child Whispers, was published.

Enid told her pupils about fairies, imps, and goblins. Their reaction to the weird and wonderful tales was a crucial gauge as to whether the stories would work in book form. "Auntie Enid", as she was known, "made everything so interesting – so much fun," Brian later wrote.

And former pupil Mollie Sayer, from Hillview, Hook Road, later confirmed this. "Everyone wanted to do everything she did because it was such fun. She was years ahead of her time."

Enid wrote in Mollie's school report: "She is a good, thoughtful, loving child. I hope I shall always keep in touch with dear little Mollie."

In 1934, Mollie went to Enid's new home in Bourne End, Bucks, to look after the author's three-year-old daughter, Gillian Baverstock. On 11th August 1997, Gillian unveiled a plaque on the wall of Southernhay dedicated to the 100th anniversary of her mother's birth.

Mollie Sayer (later Barrett) at her home, Hillview, 241 Hook Road, in 1976. Note the Noddy-patterned curtains in her nursery schoolroom.

Enid Blyton at Southernhay, Hook, with back row, left to right, Brian Thompson, David Thompson, John Terry and, front row, twins Peter and John Thompson and Mollie Sayer. Mollie later ran a nursery school, Blyton-style, at Hillview, the house on Hook Road she lived in until she retired in about 1980. Brian became chairman of the Leicester Mercury in later life. David ran Walton Park Nurseries at Hersham for many years before retiring to the West Country where he died in the mid 1990s. John Thompson, also a nurseryman, was living at Shamley Green, Guildford, in retirement. John, who attributed his love of nature to Enid Blyton, attended the plaque ceremony at Southernhay on Monday 11th August 1997, commemorating the 100th anniversary of the author's birth.

Inside Pointer's store. Above the fridge are Libby's Californian asparagus tips.

Pointer's store employed a number of loyal staff including Edward Evans, of Rose Bank, Clayton Road, far right, who served for many years. A Mr Bushell is also recalled by many in post-war years.

Wonderful smell of baked bread
Pointer's bakery

ASK any old Hook resident what they remember most about the village's past and they nearly always reply: "Pointer's bread". The bakery and general stores – and formerly the post office – was the hub of life in Hook. And on a Sunday afternoon, the air for seemingly miles around was filled with the smell of freshly baked loaves.

Many would queue at the side door for bread straight from the oven. Even at midnight, people late home from an evening out would stop off for hot rolls from the bakehouse. Local deliveries were made by horse and cart and for many years one of the delivery men was Jim Mepham. The stores closed in the 1960s and the premises, at 320 Hook Road, were taken over by the National Westminster bank.

Jim, Steve and Phil Mepham (above) all worked for Pointer's at some stage. Customers gave milkman Jim a trap for his horse, Lulu, upon retirement.

Phil Mepham lived at 302 Hook Road while working at Pointer's. His Triumph speed twin bike "did 100 on the Mickleham bends."

The grocery store stocked specialities such as loose peel, sultanas, currants and citrus peel.

Kathleen Bowyer, a regular customer from Bramham Gardens in the 1960s, later reminisced: "Sugar was weighed and placed in blue bags and a similar method was used for dried fruit."

The bacon slicer is fondly remembered by others.

Phil Mepham worked at the bakery in the late 1940s and his delivery round extended beyond the Maypole public house into Surbiton.

Once, Phil looked after brother George's black Alsatian for a time and tied him to railings at Pointer's. When people went round the back, the dog, Prince, would go mad and drag the kennel across the yard.

Our Losses Are 330,000—But Britain Does Not Flinch.

DAILY SKETCH.

GUARANTEED DAILY NETT SALE MORE THAN 1,000,000 COPIES.

No. 1,992.   LONDON, WEDNESDAY, JULY 28, 1915.   [Registered as a Newspaper.]   ONE HALFPENNY.

HOW THE WAR COMES HOME TO THE COUNTRYSIDE.

The dairyman has gone to the war.

...that that is left of the village manhood—one is an old soldier, the other a National Reservist.

The village newsagent's wife now sells the papers. Thos. Seymour (inset), the newsagent, is on service.

The women of the village all have husbands, sons, or brothers fighting at the front or in training for active service.

These three brothers, Owen, Graham, and Harold Loe are respectively in the Royal Engineers, Royal Artillery, and Black Watch.

The parson's wife and daughter help with the parish work. He is an Army chaplain.

Mrs. Bashford does the work of her husband (inset), now a private in the East Surrey Regiment.

Henry Keene is with the Army Service Corps, and his two sons, Charles and George, are also with the colours.

The war's effect on the countryside is nowhere more strikingly illustrated than in the little Surrey village of Hook, near Surbiton. There is not a slacker in the district, for the simple reason that every man, married and single, of military age has joined the Army. Only women and children and some old men are left. In the matter of patriotism the little villages have set a splendid example to the big towns.—(*Daily Sketch* Photographs.)

Hook was front-page news on 28th July 1915 when the Daily Sketch focused on how all eligible menfolk in one small, rural village had gone off to fight in the Great War. That village was Hook. The women, including newsagent Mrs Ethel Seymour, top right, were left behind to carry on their husbands' work. Also in the pictures are Henry Keene of Elm Road and his two sons, Charles and George, plus three Loe brothers.

Mrs G Bird unveils the memorial to the men of Hook who died in the First World War. The vicar, Reverend Cuthbert Harrison, far right, reads a lesson at the ceremony on 26th September 1920. The scouts played the Last Post on their bugles.

Unveiling of the war memorial, 1920

THERE are no slackers in the district, the *Daily Sketch* wrote of Hook on its front page of 28th July 1915.

'The war's effect on the countryside is nowhere more strikingly illustrated than in the little Surrey village of Hook near Surbiton.

'There is not a slacker in the district, for the simple reason that every man, married and single, of military age, has joined the Army.

'Only women and children and some old men are left. In the matter of patriotism, the little villages have set a splendid example to the big towns.'

The newspaper carried a picture of the wife of newsagent Thomas Seymour who had gone off to fight. It shows her selling newspapers to a young customer outside her store on the Hook Road, now premises at the corner of the Hook Road and the Kingston bypass. The bypass road was not in existence when this photo was taken.

Another illustration is of Mrs Bashford, left behind to plough the fields.

One picture shows two men who remain in Hook. The caption reads: 'All that is left of the village manhood – one is an old soldier, the other a National Reservist'.

Even the vicar has gone to war, as an Army chaplain. A further picture shows the wife and daughter of Reverend Cuthbert Harrison who are 'helping with the parish work'.

In 1920, the names of 42 men were listed on a war memorial unveiled at St Paul's Church, close to the site of the original Hook Church. It is seen today by the many people walking along the Hook Road.

![Seymour's newsagents shop front with NEWS OF THE WORLD BEST WEEKLY PAPER and T. SEYMOUR NEWSAGENT & TOBACCONIST signage; a family stands outside the shop](shopfront)

Seymour's newsagents, Hook Road, Southborough, c1929. Thomas Seymour jnr, outside his family's shop with siblings Doris, born 1915, Joan, born 1925, and baby Jack, born 1927.

Hook born and bred

Seymour's shop

Tom Seymour jnr, c1930, at his father's Hook Road store. Behind him, a billboard advertises racing tips in the third edition of the evening paper, The Star. Tom's sister, Doris, married nurseryman Aris Slingerland and in 1997 was living in Clayton Road. Tom lived at Ripon Gardens, Hook, with his wife, Doris, until his death on 20th September 1997.

Tom jnr in 1990.

The shops at Southborough in about 1913. On the left is Thomas Seymour's newsagent's. Next door is Arthur Farnell's shop. He sold cheese, bacon and other provisions. Then there was Ella Brooker's. She traded in drapery and millinery and was a "prim, no-nonsense sort." Last in the row was Aggas's boot and shoe shop. Walter Aggas and his son, Ron, were well-known Hook characters.

Cecil Lodge

After Hook Road was turnpiked c1811, with a tollgate at the Maypole, and much of Surbiton Common enclosed at Hook, several large houses were built including Cecil Lodge, formerly Belfield House, (both above). It stood where Cecil Close is today. Over the road, Orchard Court had gardens stretching down to Elm Road and Orchard Gardens.

Surbiton golf club and the Waffrons

Famous Welsh golfer Dai Rees (above) was assistant pro from 1934-8 and lodged with Jim Coleman and his wife at Clayton Road for £1 a week. He earned 25s a week at the club.

A H Lisner, who leased Waffrons Farm, Woodstock Lane, planned 'The Waffrons' golf course which opened on 8th June 1895. Months later, its name changed to Surbiton Golf Course. In 1912, the clubhouse was burnt to the ground, possibly by suffragettes. A new clubhouse was again razed by fire in 1921 and a thatched replacement (above) was destroyed in 1931. Jim Coleman, (inset) for many years of 66 Clayton Road, was the professional from c1912 to 1962. He died in 1963.

Middleton's laundry

Middleton's staff on an outing in bygone times. The original Southborough Arms is behind the coach. This was a working man's pub with sawdust on the floor. It also sold vegetables.

Two laundries in the Hook Road provided employment for dozens of Hook people until their closure in the 1960s. The Middleton's workforce in the early sixties numbered 50 or more. Plenty of women were taken on to sort garments into sections – non-drip, colour and dirty overalls. "Granny Middleton" lived in a big house at the front. The laundry had several acres of grounds. Some were sold for the Verona Drive and Kent Way housing estate in 1945. Nash's Maythorne laundry (far right) was near today's Southborough School.

Chessington Court Farm

BEFORE the Holmwood Road council estate was built in the early 1950s, acres of flowers and vegetables grew in this part of Hook.

Chessington Court Farm, opposite the White Hart, will be remembered for its fields of chrysanthemums, azaleas, potatoes, marrows and strawberries – and the dozen or more 100ft glasshouses in which thousands of tomato plants were cultivated.

The flowers went daily up to Covent Garden in London and in summer, local children would arrive at 3am to help harvest the strawberries so they could be taken to the capital's markets.

Chessington Court Farm, which dated back to the 18th or early 19th century, was purchased by Surbiton Borough Council and demolished in 1950 to make way

Reg Driver started work at Chessington Court Farm in 1934, earning 10s (50p) a week.

for much-needed council homes offering inexpensive accommodation.

For years afterwards, stray marrow seeds used to grow in the hedges along the Hook Road – the only visible reminder of the farm days in Hook.

The market garden was run in the 1930s by Walter Moon, son of Charlie Moon of Manor Farm, Clayton Road. Walter was the grandson of Thomas Moon who arrived in Hook in 1884 and ran Manor Farm's dairy.

At Chessington Court, in addition to the greenhouses, there was a blacksmith's workshop and a barn from which a devoted farm labourer, Mrs Bashford, once sold produce.

Reg Driver, born in Haycroft Road in 1919, worked for Walter Moon. In retirement at Shere Close, he recalled: "Four big containers used to arrive each year from Belgium with azaleas in them. All the various cut flowers for sprays went to Covent Garden, but potatoes, onions, lettuce and the like were sold from the barn.

"I used to get the men's beers from the White Hart at 12.50pm each day. It was 4d a pint. Reg Roberts, the salesman, used to have a quart of light. That came to 1s 2d (6p)."

In 1894, a labourer from Kingston was fined five shillings for stealing a quantity of turnip tops from the farm. He was seen by a policeman's son to be concealing them under his coat.

Chessington Court Farm, Hook, in May 1950, shortly before it was bulldozed. Reg Driver lived here with Walter Moon's family in 1947 and was re-housed in Shere Close when the council pulled down the farm and built the Holmwood Road and Frimley Road estate.

A track across the farm to the White Hart.

The barn from which vegetables were sold.

Family life in Hook Road

BILL Mutimer came to Hook in 1925 at the age of six and lived at Kuldana, 289 Hook Road, with his parents and two brothers, Jim, and Ernest, together with sister, Joan. He had such happy and vivid memories of his early years in the village that in 1989, he wrote them down.

Sadly, in the summer of 1997, Bill died at his home in Station Road, Chessington, but before he passed away, he said he would have great pleasure in others sharing his colourful memories.

Kuldana was named after a place in the Himalayan foothills, where Bill's father was stationed in the 1914-18 war. The family had moved to Hook from Warwick Grove in Surbiton. The large house, close to the North Star, and demolished in the mid 1960s to make way for an extension to a playground at St Paul's School, was one of a small row to be pulled down.

After settling in to his new surroundings, Bill transferred from St Andrew's School, Surbiton, to St Paul's next door.

'Arthur Harrold was the headmaster and the pupils named him Daddy Harrold,' wrote Bill. 'I feel this was more in the way of a compliment than being derisory since he was a kind and caring man. My father said he should have been a parson, not a schoolmaster.

'While at school, I recall a number of incidents. Orchard Gardens was an impassable muddy track in winter unless it frosted over. Jim and I had piano lessons in Elm Road, our tutor being a Mrs Farrow.

Young Bill Mutimer outside Kuldana, Hook Road, Hook. It was demolished in the 1960s to make way for the extension to St Paul's School playground.

Ernest and Winifred Mutimer with their children, Jim, Bill, Joan and Ernest jnr c1936.

The easiest way to Elm Road was not via Hook Road but by way of Orchard Road and Orchard Gardens, so we welcomed weather which allowed us to use this short cut.

'From our bedroom window, we once saw a car fork right into Orchard Gardens and, as it was early spring, we wondered how far it would get. It reached about half way and all the efforts of the two occupants could not shift it. As we came out of school for what was then our dinner break, a number of the children spotted two men trying in vain to get the car out of the bog. Eventually a dozen of us dashed up to help. After putting a lot of twigs under the wheels and all pushing hard, we got the car into Elm Road. We were rewarded by a handful of coins being thrown into the air – plus a smack or two when we got home with muddy boots.

Gosbury Hill was occupied by the Ricardo family at the time and I think Mr Ricardo knew the face of every pupil at the school. He was a respected friend who frequently gave parties for the children at Gosbury Hill House.

'Under age, I was allowed to join Hook Cub Scouts because my brother belonged, being one year older than me. The cubs met initially at the Haven, Hook Road, Southborough.'

The Haven was used for Hook social events, extra needlework lessons for schoolchildren and as coffee rooms and a centre for the working class to meet in. It was for years linked to St Paul's Church.

The building, today 268 and 270 Hook Road, was used in modern times by I L Brock and Co., insurance brokers. In the past it also served up 'lovely rich soup made with good meat', according to Evelyn Franklin, in an interview with the *Kingston Borough News* while she lived at 16 Haycroft Road, Hook, in 1973.

It also offered lodgings for tuppence. A slate club was run there as well and the Girls Friendly Society meetings, she said.

Bill Mutimer recalled that when he went to cub meetings at The Haven, the Kingston bypass was still under construction nearby. The cubs switched to Hook Parish Hall after it opened in 1926 and became the main centre for the village's social activities.

POW camp, 1946

German and Italian prisoners of war were kept at a camp on the site of Hook Community Centre from 1946 to 1948. At the end of this period the brown-uniformed men were given more freedom and some earned pocket money washing cars or gardening. Some tidied the grounds of St Paul's Church. Impression by Gordon Rex Houle.

The Mutimer boys' friend, Betty Matthews, aged 8, at 266 Hook Road, after a record blizzard on Boxing Day 1927. Upon marrying, she became Betty Smith. She moved to this bungalow in 1925 with her family and they had walked from their former home in Douglas Road, Tolworth. In the autumn of 1997, Betty was still here.

Fields of poppies and daisies

Orchards galore

JIM Mutimer's abiding memory of Hook is of the breathtaking beauty of the countryside around the village in the late 1920s.

Years later he wrote of those days with great fondness.

'I learned of the seasons, of the deafening beauty of the dawn chorus from our garden, the froth of blackthorn lining all the roads and the bursting of life and colour everywhere.

'I remember vividly the long hot days of summer, the scent of newly-mown hay and helping in the fields. There was the rich long grass, filled with poppies and dog daisies which we picked by the armful and, in autumn, the yield of over-abundance of rich pickings – mushrooms, apples, blackberries, chestnuts, cobnuts, hips and haws, ripe corn, oats and barley. The earth seemed to burst with goodness.

'In cold winters

Jim Mutimer.

we would go tobogganing or skating on the many ponds around, including the one we called the bluey which became the site for the Gala cosmetics factory on Hook Rise. There were two ponds in Clayton Road, one near Oaklands and the other towards the back of Pointer's.

'We certainly never went short of tadpoles in spring and had many a crafty swim in the buff – drying ourselves on our vests afterwards.

'Our kitchen was the old-fashioned type with a scullery and gas stove in it and a huge boiler for washing clothes. There was a range with a fire and oven. It was blackened until it shone.

'Mother put the washing through an old-style mangle turned by hand. How the women worked then, from dawn until bedtime.

'We had a long garden with fruit trees everywhere and what a colour they made when in blossom at springtime. There was a cooking apple tree that always gave fruit the size of grapefruits. Then came a Blenheim orange apple tree and for half way up the trunk it was completely hollow.

'A tawny owl used to call from it at night and it was only about 20 feet from my bedroom window. There were pear, plum, damson and cherry trees, too. The apples were kept in the shed and seemed to last forever. From our back window, we could see the Epsom Grandstand.

'Next door-but-one was a chicken farm so we used to go there when we needed eggs. They would still be warm from the nest.

'Opposite was a small bakery – Moores – so our bread was always hot and fresh, straight from the oven.

'There were no insecticides then but our garden always flourished, no doubt from the horse manure we'd pick up from the roads in a four-wheeled box cart. We got sixpence (just over 2p) for every full load and could find that amount in about half a mile or less.

'Behind the bakery, before the Somerset Avenue estate was built in the early 1930s, was an orchard from which I was chased many a time by the irate owner, named by us as Old Man Phipps. He spoke with the affliction that causes people to speak through their noses. We rarely did any scrumpying in the orchard. We simply used it for games of cowboys and Indians and tree climbing.

'Don Lewis, one of the baker's sons, was up a tree with us in the orchard when suddenly Old Man Phipps appeared, shouting and waving a stick. Don fell out of the tree and broke his arm. We all ran off, Don with us, crying and nursing his arm. The poor old man never caught up with us once, but if he had, he would have laid about us with a stick.

'There was a sleeper track at the top of Orchard Road and at night we would hear the clip clop of a pony and trap taking a

happy Mr Fields back to his house from the North Star without much help from its owner.'

Later in life, Bill and Jim both had dramatic times during the Second World War. Soldier Jim was taken prisoner of war by the Japanese and Bill, who served in the Navy, became a prisoner of the Germans and lost an arm after the vessel in which he was serving was sunk by German battle cruisers Gneisenov and Schornhorst.

In March 1941, the *Surrey Comet* reported on fears that William Mutimer was dead.

Bill recalled: "My mother received 43 letters of condolence. Like the proverbial penny, I turned up again and my mother received three letters of congratulations."

A red light permanently flashed on the Hook roundabout.

Kingston bypass opens

THE coming of the Kingston bypass to Hook in the late 1920s had a major impact on the community. It made the district much more accessible from London and sparked a massive boom in house-building. Owners of Hook farmland were presented with temptations too great to resist as developers drew up plans for large housing estates.

The bypass was officially opened on 28th October 1927 by the Prime Minister, Stanley Baldwin, near Raynes Park. In his address, he beseeched people "not to defile the road with ugly buildings or to use hoggish behaviour". If they did, they should be banned from using decent clubs.

Enid Blyton's pupils, the Thompson brothers, used to walk up to the road-works to see the progress being made. Thereafter, watching motor cars use the new road became the main Sunday afternoon pastime of local children. A permanently flashing red warning light was erected on the roundabout; invaluable in later smogs.

In December 1928, the new junction claimed one of its first casualties of a road accident – Lord Beaverbrook. His injuries were tended to by the Ace of Spades garage staff and his motor taken in for repair in the garage's workshops.

In 1937, Max Baer, the American heavyweight boxer, made the Ace of Spades roadhouse his training camp and gave displays to the public and celebrity visitors. The roadhouse's swimming pool was also available for public use.

Ailing king passes through Hook

King George V passes the Ace of Spades in a motor ambulance watched by villagers.

A MOTOR ambulance carrying ailing King George V to his convalescence at Craigwell House, Aldwick, Bognor, passed the Ace of Spades roadhouse in the freezing February of 1929 – three years after the General Strike.

The king died in 1936 as Bognor gained its Regis title.

The Ace of Spades was named after the firm which ran the establishment – the Ace of Spades Petroleum Company. The garage offered Ace 1, Ace 2 and Ace 3 grades of its own brand petrol.

The roadhouse patronage came from those using the new bypass. One regular patron was Britain's most courageous war-flier, Douglas Bader. On several occasions in the early 1930s, he took his girlfriend, Thelma, to the Ace of Spades for scrambled egg and bacon, or a curry.

One day, while reeling from the £68 bill for work on his MG, he drove in it with Thelma to the roadhouse. They sat grumpily at their usual table in the olde worlde barn atmosphere and listened to a tinkling piano being played next to the tiny dance floor. Outside, coloured lights illuminated the swimming pool. They decided to dance, and as they came off the upstairs dance floor, the pianist struck into Stormy Weather. Thelma told him it was very apt.

Bader lost his legs in a flying accident in 1931 but learnt to fly again, using artificial limbs. He became a wing commander in the Second World War.

HOOK Road and the new "Hooklands" Somerset Avenue estate, pictured above in about 1933. Many of the homes on the new Ransom's development, built on part of Charles Moon's dairy farm fields, were by now occupied.

In the bottom right-hand corner is the large house, Ennadale, and its garden. This was the home of aviation pioneer Harry Hawker who died in a light air-craft crash on 12th July 1921. The house was later demolished and a row of modern-style semi-detached homes was built on the site. They are named Hawkhurst Gardens – a corruption of "Hawker's Gardens". A resident of one of those houses in more modern decades was school 'lollipop' lady Shirley Davidson, a stalwart supporter of St Paul's School.

The North Star is in the bottom right hand corner. The large houses between the pub and Orchard Road – also later demolished – included Kuldana, home of the Mutimer family, and the home of the Whiteheads, who became well-known Surbiton jewellers.

Opposite was Moore's bakery, two doors down from Victory Garage, later Jack Brabham's garage.

Flying bomb hits Hook

IN JUNE 1944 Hitler unleashed his new terror weapon – the V-1 flying bomb, or doodlebug. And the first victims of this lethal weapon in the borough of Surbiton were residents of Whitehall Crescent, Hook.

Three people were killed as a row of bungalows was demolished by the blast at about 6am on Saturday 17th June 1944. The dead included an elderly woman and the parents of two young boys.

Later that day, 12 were killed at Tolworth Park Road in nearby Tolworth by another doodlebug.

Most families in Whitehall Crescent and part of Clayton Road were rendered homeless until their bugalows and houses were rebuilt over the following two years. They had to move away to emergency accommodation or go and live with friends or relations up and down the country.

Mrs Alice Vaughan of no. 8 had been aware that new perils were in the air. The previous day, an air-raid warning had sounded as she was returning from taking her five-year-old son, Brian, to Moor Lane School. With her two-year-old daughter, Brenda, in the pram, she hurried along the Hook Road in a bid to get home and take shelter. Crossing the sky, she saw one of these new pilotless planes.

Her refuge was a concrete and steel reinforced shelter her husband, Albert, had constructed for the family before he left for a distinguished service in the Royal Marines on the Orkney Isles.

The Friday bomb did not cause damage locally, but it was enough to raise

Whitehall Crescent in wartime: Albert Vaughan, his mother, Gertrude, centre, and mother-in-law Emily Hawes.

awareness of the dark days likely to lie ahead. Mrs Vaughan tried to carry on as normal that evening by making dresses for little Brenda. She placed a table in position in the lounge should a sudden alert not give her time to take the family to the garden shelter.

Later that night, the Vaughans, together with Albert's mother, Gertrude, huddled together in the shelter fearing a new attack after another air raid sounded earlier in the night.

Several hours later, the family's worst fears came true. "We heard a crash and that was it. I climbed out of the Anderson shelter, came indoors to get some clothes for the children because all they had were pyjamas, and fell down a trap door because the cover

had been blown off" recalled Mrs Vaughan, still living with Albert in the same bungalow 53 years later.

"Our daughter's cot was reduced to matchwood."

A piano in the lounge was smashed to smithereens. The family were rehoused by the council in Warren Drive, Tolworth, but lived for the first year in Burnley with relatives until the bungalow was rebuilt three years later.

Next door to the Vaughans, the Fields at no. 6 survived a terrible ordeal. Mr Field was at work with the post office but his wife was caught in the explosion and was feared dead under the debris. However, she was found alive, pinned down by a roof beam. Her kitchen had "turned sideways", the stove was still switched on and a pot of porridge had boiled dry.

At no. 4, the roof had lifted and smashed to the ground. On the roof were three young boys. They had just been been orphaned. Caleb Arthur Turnham, 30, and Edith Annie Turnham, who had been in their kitchen making tea at the time of the blast, were killed.

At no. 2, two elderly women were seriously hurt. One, 82-year-old Miss Marian Sanford, was certified dead when discovered under masonry at 7am. All three deceased were removed to Surbiton Mortuary in Lower Marsh Lane, Kingston.

Survivors were offered £350 from the authorities towards replacing furniture destroyed. Some furniture was put into storage in an empty shop unit in the newly-built North Parade in Chessington.

Houses in Clayton Road took the full force of the flying bomb blast. Although badly damaged they were extensively rebuilt enabling families to move back in.

Several bungalows were demolished in Whitehall Crescent and it was in this cul-de-sac, built only five years earlier, that three people were killed in the blast on 17th June 1944.

Doodlebug damage: the wreckage in Clayton Road and Whitehall Crescent, Hook, after the dawn strike which killed three people.

Sporting Hook

CRICKET has been played in Hook since at least 1870 when the first club was established. At first only occasional games were played on Tuesdays on a field opposite the Lucky Rover, next to Orchard Court.

For nearly a century matches have been held on the King Edward Recreation Ground. After a long battle with various councils, the Hook and Southborough Club secured a properly equipped pavilion in 1960. Prior to this players had been forced to make do with washing in buckets as the club had no running water.

The sound of leather on willow has long been a favourite summer sound in Hook as people stroll under the shade of trees on the recreation ground, opened in 1901 and named after the new king Edward VII.

Names such as Norman Jackson, Eric Taylor, David Tucker, Paul Taylor, Steve Tucker, Robert Whittingham, Fred Clark, Roy Davies and Teddy Morgan are among a list of those who have contributed to the club over the years.

The long-established Hook and Southborough Bowling Club celebrated the opening of a new clubhouse in 1997 on the Kelvin Grove side of the playing fields.

In the 1970s, The Hook and Kingston Sports Association took over land originally used for allotments and in the wartime, private pig clubs. The allotments association, originally formed in 1895, is still active beyond this site.

Hook Youth football league was formed in 1975-6 and had 23 teams in 1997. The original Hook Football club amalgamated with Chessington, retaining both names, and playsed at Chalky Lane in modern times.

Hook and Southborough Cricket Club in the early 1920s. In the top row, left to right, are Messrs Johnny Wyatt, Farrenden, Tommy Kennedy, Sole, Howard Lacey, Bernard Wilkins, Sole and Durham. Bottom row is H Denny, Vic Simmons, (later played for Sussex County), Tom Seymour, Ernie Newman and 'Smudger' Smith.

Hook Football Club in the 1919-1920 season.
The mascot with the ball is young Tom Seymour.
In the back row, left to right, are Anderson, (the trainer), 'Niffy' Maryan, George Piggot, Bernard Wilkins, 'Perce' Welbelove, Arthur Fielder and Tom Seymour snr.
In the front row are, left to right, Jack Ravenhill, Arthur Swell, Nat Longhurst, Percy Wyatt, Robert Slade, Arthur Pownall, Will Burrows and keen supporter, Alan Charman, holding a rattle.
In the background, behind the bare-branched trees of winter, can just be made out two large houses on Hook Road – Brocket, left, and Southernhay.
George Piggot worked on the brickfields at Tolworth; Bernard Wilkins was a schoolteacher and Jack Ravenhill worked at the Royal Mills, Esher.
Alan Charman, the team's biggest fan, "used to shout his head off," Tom Seymour jnr recalled in 1997.
"He was a great character", said Tom.
Percy Wyatt's father, Johnny, is in the photograph, right.

Hawker's car bedecked in flowers, the coffin passing his house in Hook Road, hordes of mourners outside St Paul's Church and, top right, an earlier photo of Harry's widow, Muriel, with daughter, Pamela. Inset: Harry Hawker.

Funeral of Harry Hawker at Hook

WORLD famous airman, Harry Hawker, lived at Ennadale, on the corner of Hook Road and Orchard Road at the time he was killed on 12th July 1921, aged just 32. The former Australian boy, whose father had dissuaded him from using pushbikes because they were "inventions of the devil" became a household name.

On arriving at Brooklands, he was taught to fly by Mr T Sopwith, and in September 1912, gained a flying certificate. Within a month he was breaking records. He pushed the altitude record up to 12,900ft, then made a 1,040-mile record flight around the British Isles in a seaplane before smashing the duration record by over three hours, staying in the air for 8 hours and 23 minutes. Ignoring the use of oxygen, he again took the record up to 24,408ft. He beat that with 27,000 ft – wearing ordinary clothes.

In 1919, with McKenzie Grieve, he set out to fly the Atlantic from Newfoundland for a Daily Mail prize. But the aircraft's engine seized up and he

The Reverend Cuthbert Harrison, of St Paul's Church, talks with a mourner, General Brancker.

came down in the sea near a small Danish boat which rescued him. For eight days, the vessel, which had no wireless, sailed the 700 miles to the Irish coast. Meanwhile, Hawker had been presumed dead. Later he received a hero's welcome.

He died while testing a Nieuport Goshawk for an aerial derby he was due to take part in. He crashed to the ground in the blazing craft near Hendon.

Hawker was buried with full honours at Hook.

The 65A to Hook – mind your heads!

"Keep your seats, please" was the cry from the conductor as the bus from Hook (North Star) went under the railway bridge in Brighton Road, Surbiton. He used to climb half way up the spiral steps at the back and make the appeal. Young mischievous boys on board sometimes threw stale cream cakes at pedestrians or had a game where they had to be the first to spot a man with a beard and shout "Beaver!" In the 1921 drought, water inspectors spied on gardeners from the top deck to see if they were illegally using hoses.

A painting of The Rhodrons in 1912.

Georgie Bird.

Man who detested cars - and was killed by one

The Rhodrons and Georgie Bird

HOOK has lost many of its grand old houses over the years including the old Vicarage (1959), Gosbury Hall (1939), Chessington Court Farm (1950) and Cecil Lodge after the last war.

Some seemed certain to still be standing well into the 21st century, however, but their acres of gardens and meadows have long since been built on. Among the survivors as the millennium approached were Orchard Court, Southernhay and Brocket House, all in Hook Road, and The Rhodrons near Elm Road.

The Rhodrons, home of a thriving social club in recent decades, was once the residence of a most colourful character – Georgie Bird. One pensioner, reminiscing with twinkling eyes, called him "a terror".

Mr Bird just could not come to terms with a new invention – the motor car. In fact, he saw red if ever one should chug past his home. His anger only increased with time and he would bare his fists at drivers of these modern modes of transport. He also blamed them for ruining his crops and put up signs telling motorists to slow down. One Friday evening in the early 1930s he was

wheeling his bicycle along the Leatherhead Road in Chessington, near Almshouse Lane, when he was in collision with a car. He was conveyed to Epsom Cottage Hospital but died some hours later.

Moments before he expired, he told his house maid, Ella Toisdivine, what happened. "I got off at every corner. I tried to dodge the brutes, but they came and hit me in the back."

Georgie Bird was born at Chessington Court Farm opposite the White Hart in 1851 and from his early boyhood days, was a keen sportsman. Being a great outdoors sort, he had a huge love for horses and was an exceptionally fine rider, the *Surrey Comet* reported.

He was a keen hunter and formed a pack of beagle hounds at a young age. He was in the Surrey Union Hunt and the Surrey Staghounds.

He kept racing horses in paddocks which were later sold and the land used for the development of the Arcade Parade shops and post office. The 11 acres were bordered by a tall hedge which stretched along Elm Road and Hook Road. Today, Rhodrons Avenue, built in the mid 1930s, recalls the heyday of the old house.

Gosbury Hill

Gosbury Hill before its demolition in the 1930s. Hundreds of homes were built by Surbiton Council on the site, forming today's Sanger Avenue, Durbin Road and The Causeway. After the war, there was a housing crisis and low-cost rented homes were highly sought after. The road named Gosbury Hill recalls the building.

HOOK'S grandest estate of the past was Gosbury Hill with its nine-acre park, private chapel, tower, farm, and two-acre orchard – all commanding fine views over the Surrey countryside.

Its house was sometimes known as Gosbury Hall or Hook Hall but it had humble beginnings. The Hall was said to have been originally a Georgian farmhouse which was extended more and more over the years until it became a hybrid collection of wings and quarters.

In 1855, a former lowly Dorset boy, who later studied hard to become a prominent London lawyer, moved in. His name was Thomas Hare. The Hare family became part of Hook's respected gentry in Victorian times and until they sold the estate in 1890, the name Hare was synonymous with Hook.

Working at the Hall as a kitchen maid in 1900 – the final complete year of Queen Victoria's reign – was 12-year-old Elsie Elson (nee Smallpiece). From her home in Frimley Road, Hook, in 1975, she recalled those "upstairs, downstairs" days.

She used to walk daily from her home in Claygate to Hook, across the fields from Manor Farm pond to the old Cricketers, and then along Clayton Road and muddy Elm Road to Gosbury Hill.

"Gosbury Hall was a lovely ancient building with a big drive sloping up to the entrance," she said. "Inside, there was a big hall and a lovely big dining room where a band used to play. It was a very beautiful place, but the servants' quarters were very poor." Mrs Elson then spent a year living in the servants' rooms. "The Hall had a chapel in it which you could get to by opening the kitchen door and going along a passage and up these stone steps, but when I was there, it was used as a billiard room," she said.

The estate at that time was owned by the Browns from Thames Ditton. "They kept a footman, a coachman and two or three housemaids. He had a housekeeper who ruled us with a rod of iron," she recalled.

Before it was pulled down in the late 1930s, the Hall was owned by the Ricardos. Lt Col Wilfrid Francis Ricardo, born 1868, became well-known in Hook. He was a keen golfer and when he won a match, celebrated by throwing chocolate bars to children in the streets as he drove home in a large grey car from nearby Surbiton golf course.

Always a festive hamper

The Ricardos

GOSBURY Hill, the luxurious estate between the top of Elm Road and Cox Lane was sold by the Hare family in September 1890.

Later owners were the Ricardo family who were much-respected in Hook. Colonel Wilfrid and Mrs Norah Ricardo took over the ownership from Mr and Mrs Isaac Bell, who used to live in Holland. Norah was Mr and Mrs Bell's eldest daughter. She married Lt Col Wilfrid Ricardo in 1904. He served in the Boer war in 1899-1900 and in the Great War.

The Ricardos had two daughters, Mary and Jan, and a son, Francis.

Mary married the Honourable Henry Hope and Jan also married and had a daughter. Jan had earlier vowed to marry Major 'Boy' Browning but owing to intervention from the families concerned, the wedding did not take place. Instead, the major married Daphne Du Maurier, the novelist.

The Ricardo family sold the estate when plans were drawn up for the railway branch line to Chessington which opened in 1938. The line was expected to run through the land. They moved to Cow Cottage, Cotterell, near Sunningdale, Berkshire, in the 1930s.

Jan died in tragic circumstances and Mrs Ricardo also lost her life in a similar tragic situation involving a train.

Head of staff at the Hall was a Mr Pulley who, in the early 1930s, left for employment with Earl Jellicoe on the Isle of Wight. It was here, in 1933, that Mr Pulley was drowned trying to save some girls who were in difficulty in the sea.

Mr Pulley's daughter, Bonny, lived for years afterwards in Orchard Road, as did his grand-daughter, Tina.

During their time at Gosbury Hill, the Ricardos often opened up their home for social occasions. They often threw parties for local children, especially at Christmas.

Many a day would youngsters wait in the street for the family to pass in their motor car and wave.

Mrs Ricardo's parents, the Bells, employed a

Sale particulars of Gosbury Hill in 1890.

A couple walk their dog across the oat fields from Moor Lane to the top of Gosbury Hill in the hot summer of 1947.

Work in progress on the council houses, 1952.

Dutchman, Jon Van-Waarde, to work for them as a farmer, valet and estate manager and arranged his relocation.

Jon's daughter, Mina, recalled years later: "Every Christmas, the Ricardos used to give us a hamper with a turkey."

The Ricardos' 13 acres included the Madonna strawberry farm, now the Orchard Road and Durbin Road area.

Mrs Ricardo had a chihuahua dog called Lizzie and two golden retrievers, Marigold and Buttercup.

Philanthropist Mr Ricardo's habit of throwing chocolate bars and sweets to the children in the street sometimes backfired when over-protective parents decided their disappointed offspring should leave the chocolate for dogs to devour.

Throughout 1948 and 1949, contractors were busy laying concrete and tarmacadam on what had been wooded countryside.

Surbiton Council's mission was to build affordable houses for the 2,500 'homeless' on its list. One of the reasons for the surge in demand was the influx of men returning from the war.

The development of the large estate forming Cox Lane, Gosbury Hill, Durbin Road, Sanger Avenue and part of Moor Lane provided work for many. The contractors used included Miles Construction Ltd of St Mark's Hill, Surbiton, Crouch of Kingston and Coates.

The houses fronting Moor Lane were mainly completed by March 1950, although work on the finishing touches was briefly hampered by a late snowfall at the end of the month.

Construction work on 300 council homes between Mansfield Road and Clayton Road was also by this time at an advanced stage with some having been occupied for at least two years.

1907

Edwardian days: some of the pupils at Hook School in 1907.

UNTIL 1859, Hook did not have its own school and education was not compulsory until 1870. Some children may well have walked into Chessington for lessons at a schoolroom on the Leatherhead Road. In 1857, St Paul's Church received an offer of land, free of charge, for use as a school at the junction of Hook Road and Orchard Road. The gift came from Walter Mercer, a former mayor of Kingston, who had strong links with Hook. The new school's foundation stone was laid on 28th July 1859, by Thomas Hare of the nearby mansion, Gosbury Hall, on Gosbury Hill. Life was tough for the poorer families in Hook and parents would encourage their young children to go fruit picking to bring in extra income. Some youngsters were up at 3am to pick strawberries in the summer and if they went to school with juice stains in their fingernails, they were sometimes caned.

NEW
SCHOOL ROOM,
HOOK.

The ROOM just finished attached to the
NATIONAL SCHOOL at HOOK, will (D.V.) be

OPENED

on TUESDAY EVENING NEXT

JUNE 6th, 1871, at half-past 7 o'clock.

Addresses to the Meeting

Will be delivered by Clergymen and others.

The Friends of Education are respectfully invited
to attend.

COLLECTION WILL BE MADE AT THE CLOSE
THE MEETING.

Hook School's new room was opened in 1871.

Children of Hook (St Paul's) School in about 1900, the last complete year of Queen Victoria's reign. The school opened in 1860.

Tom's school

T OM Seymour will be remembered as one of Hook's best known characters, having spent all of his life in the locality.

He was born on September 14th 1909 into a family of newsagents at the corner of Hook Road and what is now the Kingston bypass. Then, much of Hook was orchards, corn fields, strawberry plantations and fruit farms.

Tom's father, Thomas Charles Seymour, and his mother, Ethel, were the only newsagents between Surbiton and Leatherhead. The rounds stretched all the way to Malden Rushett and newspaper boys such as Ted Moore, born 1908, would set up a relay with young Tom who would cycle as far as Almshouse Lane in Chessington and pass on a batch of newspapers to Ted to deliver to 34 homes

Thomas and Ethel Seymour certainly had their hands full, trying to raise not only Tom but three other children – Doris, born in 1915, Joan, born in 1925 and Jack, born handicapped in 1927.

During the First World War, Thomas snr left Hook, along with most other Hook men, to serve abroad. He was sent to Egypt with the Royal Army Ordnance

Year the school was built.

Hook School, Orchard Road, in 1922 with teacher Miss Olive May Taylor on the far right.

Corps. Mrs Seymour ran the business in his absence and found time to feed little Tom when he came home from Hook school for midday lunches of stew, sausages, bacon pudding, or, on Mondays, "burn-a-hole-in-the-frying-pan" bubble and squeak.

As an 87-year-old man, living in flats at Ripon Gardens, Hook, Tom said he did not enjoy his schooldays. He preferred to be out and about delivering newspapers for his parents. His customers included the Thompsons, of Southernhay, at the time Enid Blyton had her first book, Child Whispers, published in 1922.

Another customer was Harry Hawker, the pioneer aviator, who lived at Ennadale on the corner of Orchard Road and Hook Road.

At Hook School, Mr George Garrett was headmaster of the junior school and his wife, Amelia, head of the infants. They took up the posts in 1902. Mr Garrett held the position until 1925 and his wife until 1922.

Mr Garrett's elderly mother lived with the couple at the school house – still standing at the end of the 20th century and carrying a brick with the date 1859 on it.

Mr Garrett had "a beard like the King, George V".

He was "quite nice but a bit of a disciplinarian".

Other staff included Mr Corner, Mr Summers, Mrs Groombridge, Miss Button and Miss Olive May Taylor – "OMT" or "Old Mother Taylor" as the pupils nicknamed her. "She was quite decent," Tom remembered.

Miss Taylor's mother and father kept a draper's shop in the Hook Road next to Vale Road. It later became a fruit shop.

In winter, Tom and his schoolpals used to go down to the pond in Clayton Road – now the site of Bramham Gardens – and slide around on the ice.

1930

Classes at Hook School in 1930. On the left at the front, next to the dark teddy, are Lilian Care and Stanley Oates. Behind them are J Batt, Tommy Miller and another teddy, behind which is Mary Bowrie. At the very back, tallest, is Marjorie Keene and in front of her, Jack Ivers. On the right, at the front, are Betty Yates and Gwen Keene. Behind them on the far right is Jeanne Moore (then Chappell).

Land of Far Beyond
Miss Rumble

MISS Joan Rumble was one of the best-known teachers at St Paul's (Hook) School. Thousands of Hook children were taught by her between 1940 and 1972. A very traditional schoolmistress, she is well remembered for her end-of-day reading of Land of Far Beyond, based on Pilgrim's Progress. This would be listened to attentively by pupils as they sipped surplus milk through straws from one-third pint bottles after a day of English, maths and spelling tests.

As a young child, Miss Rumble moved to Portsmouth where her father had secured a job in the Admiralty depot in Gosport. But he soon became seriously ill and her mother faced a tough time trying to make ends meet. When he died in 1924 there was no pension for civil servants' widows. Joan was only 10.

An older girl, Betty Preston, living next door to the Rumbles provided much-needed friendship and help. Although remaining in the Portsmouth and Isle of Wight area for all of her life, Betty became a dear friend of Miss Rumble's for some 80 years.

As a schoolgirl, Miss Rumble moved to Kingston where her godmother lived and it was arranged for her to go to Tiffins. grammar school. She became a prefect and "wore an enamel badge with three fishes on it".

Later she trained at Brighton to become a teacher. These were two of the happiest years of her life.

Her first post was in a new school at Hackbridge near Wallington. This involved a "beastly journey" from the Kingston area, changing trains three times.

So when a position arose at Hook School in about 1940, just after the start of the war, Miss Rumble jumped at it. The headmaster, Arthur Harrold, who had held the post since 1925, was to work alongside Miss Rumble for another six years. The Harrold family, who lived in Thornhill Road, were closely involved with St Paul's Church for many years and Arthur's daughter, Sarah, married Hugh Featherstone, only son of Reverend William Featherstone, vicar of Hook who died in 1944. Sarah died after the

Miss Rumble with the class of 1969. She always felt that the majority of Hook children were "friendly, clean and well-behaved".

birth of her younger daughter and Hugh died a few years later. The two orphaned daughters were brought up by Arthur Harrold and his wife, Mary.

In the war, Miss Rumble sometimes taught in one of the five air- raid shelters in the playground. "I would be reading Just William and I'd have to stop until after the raid and the boys would then plead 'carry on!'", Miss Rumble reminisced.

After Mr Harrold's retirement in July 1946, Mr E C Beaven took over the headship. Many years later, in retirement, Miss Rumble recalled: " He was a lovely person. He had that school in the

palm of his hand. He used to do all the dinner duty himself and take the children up to the parish hall for their meals. When inspectors came round, they met him and were so satisfied they did not bother looking around."

Miss Rumble was remembered by one former pupil who said: "She always used to read Land of Far Beyond or The Secret Garden. She often wore a paisley neckscarf and part of her blackboard had light green lines for practising handwriting."

In the autumn of 1997, Miss Rumble was living at Moray House, Adelaide Road, Surbiton.

This was Mr Clark's class in the summer of 1969. In October 1995, ex-pupil Lee Giller organised a reunion party at the school and persuaded their former headmaster Stan Lacey to take assembly before a joyful buffet at the North Star. Remarkably, all but four turned up and Mr Lacey was very moved by the way everyone got on so well at the event. One, Sian Ackroyd, formerly of Cox Lane, flew over from Switzerland.

Memories of a former pupil

WENDY Muir attended St Paul's School 1943-9. Fifty years on, she wrote: "Miss Stowville was our teacher and I can remember her in tears at her retirement. I did not realise until then that grown-ups cried.

'Our classroom, Infants A, was separated from Infants B by a heavy, wooden, concertina screen with frosted glass panels.

'There were no hand basins in the toilets those days. At first, Mr Harrold was the head and we were taught by his daughter, Sarah.

'The hut at the back of the British Restaurant at the Parish Hall was a classroom in 1946– the year I spent four weeks in Tolworth Isolation Hospital with scarlet fever. All my toys had to be fumigated and my books destroyed.

'My teachers included Miss Rumble and Mr Clark. During the summer of 1944, I was evacuated to Somerset at the time of the flying bombs.

'In the notoriously cold winter of 1947, I was in the hut and the only heating was a coke stove at one end where we would put the one-third pint bottles of milk to defrost.'

Mr Clark's class, spring 1967

THIS contented class enjoyed some happy days at St Paul's. Many of the pupils enjoyed summer camps in Snowdonia led by headmaster Stan Lacey and Bill Bellerby, head of Knollmead, Tolworth.

In their earlier years, most witnessed the widening of the Hook Road to dual carriageway in 1963-4, the opening of the school pool in 1963 and the new hall which meant they no longer had to walk to the parish hall for school dinners.

On their way home the youngsters would perhaps have stopped off at A C Benn's sweet shop for black jacks (eight for a penny) or Trebor's fruit salads. Alternatively, aniseed balls and jamboree bags were favourites. Another little sweet shop next to Benn's on the church side of Hook Road also had a selection of goodies.

Some may have read the Beano or Dandy while waiting for a haircut at elderly Mr Chappell's salon behind Benn's.

Top row, left to right: Yvonne Izard, Morag McIndoe, Janice Nightingale, Kay McIntyre, Janet Maynard, Stephanie Creton, and Gwyneth Jones. Second row from top: Paul Butterick, Mark Davison, Malcolm Field, John Muggleton, David Philpott, Fred Smith and Alan Hilder. Middle row: Michael Love, Michael Redknap, Paul Taylor, Mark Adams, Paul Thacker, Stephen Bull and Steven Death. Second row from bottom: Sarah Ling, Chrisitine Defty, Kim Hunt, Pauline Wilson, Joan Eales, Gwen Mewburn and Lindsay Amer. Bottom row: Philip Butler, Derek Mullins, Gordon Bayliss, Stephen Saunders, and the Blackmore twins.

School dinner lady Freda Baker made delicious butterscotch tarts.

'Class of 1967' St Paul's Hook

In 1963 – the year of the Beatles' first LP – there was a far more important event on the calendar. For on Saturday 15th June, the Olympic swimmer Elizabeth Long opened the new swimming pool at St Paul's School. Headmaster Stan Lacey, right, made a speech.

The things children say

Young children remember the most curious things about their schooldays and their teachers. Former pupils at the notably friendly St Paul's School, Hook, have a colourful assortment of recollections.

Mrs Nora Collins was in charge of the six-year-olds at St Paul's School, from about 1948 to 1971. She had previously taught for several years in India, where her husband was an Army instructor. She had two daughters who lived in Yorkshire.

Mrs Collins will be remembered by many of her pupils for her green, floral, chiffon-type housecoat which was tied at the neck with a bow. She also wore a variety of floral dresses which, it is understood, she made herself.

Mrs Doreen Stone, deputy head during her 21 years' service up to 1984, was remembered for her black leather coat and smart fashion sense.

Children were saddened when her husband, a respected pianist died. Mrs Stone carried on living in Hook for many years at Tudor Close off Moor Lane.

Ex-pupils recall Stan Lacey, headmaster from 1960 to 1976, always carrying a green ball-point pen in his breast pocket.

Mr Lacey was a Leicestershire man who lived with his wife, Mavis, son, Richard, and daughter, Judith, in Somerset Avenue before they moved to 3 Kelvin Grove. After retiring from Tolworth's Grand Avenue School at Easter 1989, Mr Lacey became a part-time postman in the 1990s, at one stage pedalling daily to Leatherhead. His usual rounds were in Hook.

Mr Lacey once ran a campaign to reduce food wastage at school dinners. An aluminum bowl containing the uneaten food was weighed and the amount written on a blackboard at the side. He played the organist at St Paul's Church.

In the sixties, Mr Dable, who lived with his wife in the adjoining schoolhouse, was 'hot' on tables and spelling. He had a large set of orange sheets he used as a prop for his lessons. He was fond of carpentry. Another teacher in the 1960s – Miss Rene Froude – lost two pairs of spectacles from bouncing netballs during playground duties.

Mrs Collins

Mrs Collins, Mr Clark, Mr Richard Pengilly, Mrs Ada Clark, and Mr Lacey with four other teachers on the right including Mrs Stone,(1963-84) Miss Rumble and Mrs Rook (far right).

Remembering Mrs Rook

Hundreds of Hook children owe their early education to Mrs Ethel Rook.

She taught the youngest classes at St Paul's School from September 1945 to her retirement in July 1972.

Mrs Rook was born on 4th April 1911.

She was raised in Southampton, one of four children. She trained at Salisbury to be a teacher and after applying for jobs, secured a post briefly at St John's Junior School, Kingston, and then a position for three years at Mitcham before coming to Hook by chance.

Her husband, Cyril, who worked for County Hall, one day met St Paul's headmaster Mr Harrold, who needed a teacher for the youngest pupils. Mr Rook said his wife was only suitable for older children. "Nonsense", replied Mr Harrold – 'If I can teach the little ones, so can she'. Mrs Rook took up the challenge at the end of the war and stayed nearly 27 years.

In active retirement at Pound Close, Long Ditton, she surprised many by her world travels well into her late eighties.

Her voyages have taken her to North America, Sweden, Norway, the Holy Land and Yugoslavia and she was planning to visit New Zealand for the millennium.

Her son, John, became head of Southborough School, Hook, in the mid 1990s. This secondary school was opened near the Ace of Spades in 1963.

Former St Paul's pupil, Sue Davison, recalled: "In Mrs Rook's class was a white statue of a goose, a green tarpaulin which covered the toys, little slates to practise writing and wooden puzzles carrying pictures of black and white cows."

Mrs Rook.

Mr Fred Clark

Mr Clark.

Fred Clark was one of St Paul's School's best-known teachers. He took up the post in 1937 at the age of 30 and the following year was acting head for a term. He retired in October 1969.

A Yorkshireman, keen footballer and cricketer, he lived in Vallis Way for many years. His widow, Ada, continued living in the house until her death in April 1997.

He first started teaching in the West Riding before he moved to a school in High Wycombe. From there he moved south to Hook. He was a key member of Hook and Southborough Cricket Club and was secretary of the Kingston and District Junior Football Association for 14 years.

In April 1967, he suffered head injuries when a lamppost fell on him in a road accident by Jack Brabham's Garage, walking to school. He spent five months hospitalised.

Petula Clark sings in Vallis Way

Residents of Vallis Way celebrated the end of war in 1945 with a party. Singer Petula Clark, of Salmons Road, Chessington, was star guest at several Hook events, including fetes at the old vicarage and on the recreation ground.

Houses were draped in bunting as families celebrated.

Moor Lane School pupil, Petula Clark, sang only three songs at the Vallis Way party owing to her recording contract.

RAF Hook balloon barrage centre during the war.

RAF Hook balloon barrage centre

IN 1938, the year Prime Minister Neville Chamberlain signed the Munich Agreement with Hitler, work began on building a barrage balloon centre on 45 acres of land on the south side of Mansfield Road.

The site had been bought in October 1937 by the Air Ministry. It was to be one of 10 such stations in and around London. These sites were to have 50 or more balloons which would trail steel cables from a height of 25,000 feet to stop raiding aircraft approaching at low heights.

Recruitment started in October 1938 for the two Territorial Air Service squadrons, 904 and 905, to be stationed at RAF No. 2 Hook balloon centre, as part of the Auxiliary Air Force rather than the regular RAF. The RAF officially took possession in August 1938.

On 16th April 1939, King George VI and Queen Elizabeth, Neville Chamberlain, and US ambassador, Joseph Kennedy, visited the centre and were met by 1,200 auxiliaries and a cheery crowd in Hook Road.

After the war, in 1945 the site became an RAF medical rehabilitation centre until closure in the 1980s and later redevelopment as a housing estate.

After being renamed RAF Chessington, in 1968 the base expanded to take in patients from all the armed services. Although inter-service rivalry had chiefly ceased, rank snobbery remained. Only patients from the lower ranks went to the rehabilitation unit. The rest were sent elsewhere.

For nearly 20 years, the base continued in this role, as a joint services medical unit.

Some characters of Hook

PC Eric Blumfield was beat bobby in the 1970s.

Bill Cole of Woodgate Avenue was known as the 'Hook and Chessington kid' because he dressed like a cowboy.

Gordon Fischel of 230 Hook Road was a German Jewish refugee and was said to have been a brilliant scientist.

Sydney Groves mended bicycles at Hook Cycles, Ace Parade, up to c1979. The shop was on the corner of Elmcroft Drive.

Hooked on Hook after all these years: Marjorie Dunford, (nee Keene); Mollie "Gill" Gillingham (nee Keene), Mina Van-Waarde, and Gwendoline Strong (also nee Keene); pictured in Gill's pretty garden at Frimley Road in July 1997.

Rev. Bill Mullenger was curate of St Paul's Church from 1974 to 1981 and a keen youth worker in the Hook parish.

A visit to the Express Cleaners in Arcade Parade was a happy experience in the 60s and 70s. Former ballet dancer Midge Macbeth, who lived in Holmwood Road, used to sit cheerfully in the window and sew. "They came in looking glum and they went out laughing," she said. When the business was sold in the early 80s, Midge had to leave her familiar spot.

June Norton started work at L E Webb's chemist's, Arcade Parade, in 1960 and stayed for 36 years, by which time she had two grown-up grandchildren. Do you recall the weighing machine outside, on which some people weighed their holiday luggage and tied dogs to? Webb's was an old-fashioned chemist's with tea chests acting as shelves.

Betty Attfield, of Ripon Gardens, buttered 144 rolls each morning at the "blind man's cafe" next to the Co-op.

Miriam Barnfield: altar flowers duty for years at St Paul's Church.

Jeanne Moore has been one of Hook's best-known personalities and worked tirelessly for St Paul's Church for more than half a century. In recognition of her service to the community, she was awarded an MBE in the mid 1990s.

Hook Underpass

First of its type in country

The underpass soon after opening.

HOOK Underpass was the first of its type in the country. Opened on 12th February 1960, it was a major engineering feat and a model of the construction has been displayed for years at the Science Museum in London.

The underpass was built to relieve the terrible traffic flow problems on the Kingston bypass at the Ace of Spades which were becoming a big headache by the late 1950s as more and more people started to own motor cars.

In its first year, the road surface was heated to ward off frost and ice. Power to the underground cable mats was supplied by generators at the roadside. However, this must have proved very costly or ineffective, for the system was soon removed.

In the great Hook storm of 6th July 1973, firemen pumped water many feet deep from the underpass. And in nearby Kelvin Grove houses were awash with water up to 4ft 6ins deep. The home of Dick and Ruby Fincham had sofas floating in chest-deep water. And outside, a rescuer used a boat to help stricken neighbours. Rainfall was 4.65ins in two hours. Some 300 homes were flooded. It was among the three heaviest downpours ever recoded in Surrey.

Life at the Ace of Spades in the 1990s was very much in the fast lane and the approach roads were given "red route" designations by the government, forbidding vehicles to stop at any time.

HK.16   The Roundabout, HOOK.

The Ace of Spades garage and the Kingston bypass in about 1951 before the Hook Underpass was built.

The "new" Southborough Arms - later the Cap in Hand – was once the site of Haycroft Farm. The farmyard extended south over what is now Kelvin Grove.

Ace Parade was built in 1938 on the site of Haycroft House. Kelvin Grove opposite was partly completed by 1934. Plans provided for a tennis court in most gardens.

Traffic congestion at the Hook roundabout by the Ace of Spades in the late 1950s. By 1959, work was well under way on the Hook Underpass which would take the A3 Kingston bypass under the roundabout, freeing the movement of cars and lorries travelling between Esher and west London. In 1976, in spite of earlier protests from environmentalists, the Esher bypass opened just west of the underpass. It carved a swath through the countryside around Kelvin Grove, Woodstock Lane South, Clayton Road, Lovelace School and the historic Grapsom site. In the 1990s, rush-hour traffic at the Ace was again a daily problem. The police phone box outside the Southborough Arms (pictured left in 1951) was a familiar Hook landmark. People requiring police assistance could use this facility. Sometimes police cadets would be at hand at this junction, directing traffic at busy times.

Celebrations in 1947 as council estate opens

Councillor Woodgate greets Clayton Road people in 1947.

Ripon Gardens, seen here in 1951, was built between Manor Farm and Scott's paddocks.

WOODGATE Avenue estate was previously fields, paddocks and raspberry bush allotments with barely a house in sight not long before the 1939-45 war. From the bedroom windows of cottages in Clayton Road, Barwell Court could be seen and the roar of lions from Chessington Zoo could be heard on still nights.

But when hostilities ceased, and life struggled to get back to normal, the open space between Mansfield Road and Clayton Road was earmarked for housing by Surbiton Council which was concerned at the huge pressure on it to build affordable homes for needy families. Some houses were built by Taylor Woodrow.

By 1947, work was at an advanced stage on a housing estate of 300 houses and 72 flats initially labelled Depot Road but later renamed Woodgate Avenue.

The name was changed because the keys to the first two completed council homes, at 35 and 37 Clayton Road, on the corner of Woodgate Avenue, were handed over in a ceremony conducted by Councillor Amy Woodgate on 8th August 1947.

Large blocks of flats at Woodgate Avenue and Ripon Gardens were nearing completion by July 1951 and Holsworthy Way, Hereford Way and Tiverton Way were occupied by the end of 1952. Devon Way and parts of Mansfield Road had already been completed by 1946 on part of Charles Moon's Manor Farm.

Councillor Woodgate handed the keys of 35 and 37 Clayton Road to two Surbiton families of ex-servicemen – Mr and Mrs J Cooke (RAF) who had four children, and Mrs VF Brenes (Army) who had five children. In the war, an ARP depot equipped with ambulances, was based at the site of Charles Lesser House.

The paddocks, which formed part of the White Hart end of the estate, formerly belonged to the Scott family from Whitehall, the large mansion on the site of Whitehall Crescent, sold by auction in July 1938. The popular Hook Youth Club formerly met in huts at Hereford Way before it transferred to Devon Way.

The Clayton family

Ace Parade

ACE PARADE was built on the site of Haycroft House and gardens which was home for many years to the eminent Clayton family.

Francis Stephen Clayton, born in London in 1829, moved to Hook in the 1850s "when his parents acquired the handsome mansion known as Haycroft, which stands surrounded by broad acres in a charmingly rural spot off the Hook Road."

During his life at Haycroft, he worked exceedingly hard for the church of St Matthew, Surbiton, but was a generous benefactor to Hook in many ways and was for a time a churchwarden at St Paul's.

He followed in the footsteps of his father, John, and worked as a solicitor at Lancaster Place, London.

Francis Stephen Clayton. His family name is recalled in Clayton Road.

This view of Ace Parade was taken on 3rd September 1962 from the junction of Elmcroft Drive and Hook Road.

Upon Francis's death in September 1912 at the age of 83, the *Surrey Comet* reported: "His tall, venerable figure was known to most of the residents around, and his genial presence will be sadly missed by all grades of local society."

The obituary continued: "So unostentatiously did Mr Clayton perform his countless acts of kindness that the full extent of his benefactions will probably never be known."

It said that no genuine case of distress in the locality passed him by, and in him "the poor of Surbiton,

Tolworth and Hook had a true friend".

A year after the construction of Ace Parade, war broke out and at one stage an Ack Ack gun was placed on the roof of the new Sainsbury's store which commanded views over the surrounding area. It had to be taken down when it threatened to cause structural damage.

Charles H Clayton – Francis's brother – was also a solicitor and lived to the age of 101, spending much of his married life at nearby Cockcrow Hill, Long Ditton, having married Lydia Hare of Gosbury Hill.

Francis S Clayton donated a drinking fountain to the new Hook recreation ground in 1906.

Hook Community Centre and Hook branch library were opened on 15th December 1961. A large fund-raising event had been organised by local people to help fund the project. The buildings were constructed on the site of the prisoners of war camp. Previously, the library was in a small building in Hartfield Road, later used by 2nd Hook scouts..

If you were walking around the shops at Hook, you may well have been 'snapped' by David Tippett Wilson of 296 Hook Road. For years he was a keen photographer of everything 'Hook'.

Life in the countryside – for less than a grand!

World Cup footballer in Hook Road

A MEMBER of England's World Cup winning football team which beat Germany in the 1966 finals, lived at the time in 323a Hook Road, next door to Orchard Court. George Cohen (left) is said to have celebrated back at the house after the triumphant game. He lived in one of the modern semi-detached houses on the site of the old vicarage, pulled down in 1959. The old vicarage was once the hub of Hook social events such as fetes and garden parties.

In 1997, Roger Finch 'came of age' as headmaster of St Paul's School. He took over from Mr Lacey in 1976.

Mrs Stonard

For more than 21 years, Doris Stonard saw pupils of St Paul's School safely across Hook Road and Orchard Road.

And when she completed 21 years' service in 1975, she was invited into assembly for a presentation. Not only that, the staff of Wallaker's estate agents in Hook Road handed her a bottle of champagne. She died suddenly in September 1976, aged 54.

Adam Faith

Hetty Hatchard taught scores of children the piano at her home in Somerset Avenue, where she had lived since the houses were built in the early 1930s. She will be remembered for her kindly manner and her dislike of bad language. She died in December 1989 aged 87. One of her pupils was singer Adam Faith but the piano did not seem to be his forte.

Countryside houses for £675

WHEN the Somerset Avenue estate was built in the early 1930s, it was possible to buy one of these stylish new homes for £675.

The estate was planned by Ransoms the builders – the family who still traded in 1997 as a plant hire firm in the same premises in Hook Road, near Mansfield Road, as they did then.

The new roads were named after places in the West Country. This was apt, for the farmland on which the homes were built had been owned by Moon's, the Hook farmer who hailed from Somerset. That is how Devon Way, Holsworthy Way and other roads obtained their names. Selwood wa an ancient Somerset forest and Vallis the name of a farm nea Frome.

The Ransom's sales brochur advertising houses on this new "Hooklands estate" as it was the known, wrote: "Hooklands is ideal ly situated for the enjoyment of country life without any inconve nience.

"There are facilities for tennis cricket, bowls and putting or Hook's own recreation ground And swimming and sunbathing may now be enjoyed at Surbiton Lagoon. Tolworth Central Schoo for children is just 10 minutes walk away."

Hunters Road's Romany gipsies

Before the houses were built in Hunters Road in the early 1930s, a clus ter of six Romany-style gipsies had a camp.

Marjorie Cherry, who moved to the road in 1934, once said: "They use to sit out at night and cook on open fires. In side their caravans, every thing seemed to be made of brass.".

J S Wood, butcher

J S Wood's, 375 Hook Road, soon after it opened in 1939. It shut in 1992.

FOR more than 50 years, J S Wood, the family butcher, traded at 375 Hook Road. The store opened on 4th July 1939 – two months before the war – and during air raids, people used to dive for cover under the open garage next door at 379 Hook Road which became A C Benn, newsagent's some years later.

Wood's other neighbour was Mrs Lineham, the haberdasher's and sub post office at no.373. At first, Mrs Wood ran an annexed grocery department next door at 377 Hook Road but there was some difficulty

J S Wood's son, Peter, with his Christmas turkeys in the 1980s.

Arcade Parade (later known as Hook Parade) in about 1962, shortly before the Hook Road was widened to a dual carriageway. The Royal Arsenal Co-operative Society department stores are next to the Midland Bank. The "blind man's cafe" was formerly on the site of the bank, built c1961.

obtaining permission because Pointer's the grocer's was already established over the road.

The first stage of Arcade Parade was built in 1938/9, about the same time as Ace Parade half a mile up the road. War then halted work and the parade 'ran out' at no. 379 (later Preedy's and Dillons' newsagents).

The continuation of work on the parade after the war and into the early 1950s enabled the Royal Arsenal Co-operative multi-department store to start trading.

Over the road, F W Woolworth's opened on

13th October 1955. Its neighbours in the early 1960s were Timothy White's, Coombe's bakery, the Maypole grocery shop, Bryants clothing and outfitters, a small self-service Bishops store, Matthew's the butcher's and Davison's off-licence (1952 to June 1996). A Ganley's, greengrocer's, was at 2 Arcade Parade and Calvin's fish shop close by.

In a type of hut, just to the rear of the bank site in the 1950s was the Copper Kettle cafe, run by a blind man, Mr Melville, and his wife. An assistant, Betty Attfield, would

prepare "mounds of egg and bacon sarnies" for the builders constructing the Bramham Gardens development in 1951/2.

Mr Melville, "a great big robust man" would always do the washing up and he liked helping to repair people's kettles.

Betty once said: "I used to soak 4lbs of haricot beans overnight and cover them with tomato sauce next morning and they were then lovely baked beans. Each morning I had to prepare and butter 12 dozen rolls." A big copper kettle advert hung outside the cafe.

Route 65 bus

AFTER almost 70 years of serving Hook, the 65 bus ceased operation south of Kingston in 1987. By this time, the service was running on Sundays only, chiefly to take visitors to Chessington World of Adventures on the zoo's busiest day.

The route commenced as route 105a in 1914 when it ran from Ealing to Leatherhead on Sundays, taking Londoners out into the countryside. From early 1920, on weekdays, the *105* was extended from Surbiton to the

Journeys up to a mile on the 65 cost 2d (less than 1p) in the sixties.

North Star, where it terminated.

Until that time, there was no bus service in Hook and people not possessing a motor car had to either cycle, hire

A 65 bus makes a stop at the Lucky Rover, Hook, on its way to Ealing in 1976. The North Star is in the distance.

a 'fly' trap or walk.

The 105 omnibus for many years only went as far as 'Hook – The North Star', beyond which there was no 'proper' tarmac-surfaced road.

The bus drivers of these open-topped vehicles used to reverse into Orchard Road and then pull up at the North Star, so they were facing the right direction for a return to Kingston and Ealing.

Arthur Matthews, of 266 Hook Road, whose daughter Betty Smith lived for more than 70 years at the same bungalow, used to cross the road to offer to put down sacks for the drivers if Orchard Road was icy in winter.

Brian Thompson, of Southernhay, Hook Road, later recalled: "All buses were open-topped. Seats were hard and in front of each was a heavy macintosh cover to pull over one's knees in the event of rain. Two corners of this cover were fastened to the seat in front, and the cover folded envelope-style so that the other two corners could be lodged when it was not in use. This fold sometimes presented a hazard because it would fill with water if the cover remained folded during rain."

A variety of characterful bus conductors, including 'Scottie' entertained passengers on the route during the sixties and seventies. One male conductor, from Holmwood Road, Hook, used to climb upstairs, whistling, and call out jokingly: "Anyone got the kettle on?"

The 65 ceased running to Leatherhead on 29th November 1968 when the 71 took over.

In the 1990s the 465 linked Kingston, Hook and Leatherhead, while Kingston could be reached also by 'hoppa'-style buses, or the 71. The 65 continued a Kingston-Ealing route only and for some years was operated by Armchair Transport.

Sainsbury's Hook branch opened at Ace Parade on 2nd July 1938 and shut on 22nd March 1980 when a superstore opened in Surbiton. When this picture was taken in 1965, the shop had been extended. In 1997, the premises were an Indian restaurant.

The 65A London Transport bus ran regularly through Hook from the mid 1960s to the late 1970s. Its full-length route was from Ealing to Chessington Zoo and its stops included the North Star, Hook Community Centre, White Hart, Bridge Road, Copt Gilders and Chessington. Some journeys, such as the one above, pictured c1971, terminated at the Bridge Road roundabout during busy periods. The 65A replaced the double-decker 265 which served Copt Gilders estate in the fifties and early sixties.

Serving St Paul's Church

Vicars – or equivalents – in charge of St Paul's Church, Hook, from 1842 up to the early 1990s: Very top right: Thomas Pyne, 1842-1873. Then, in a downwards spiral: William Clarke, 1877-1890; Charles Block, 1890-1902; Walter Dingwall, 1903-1906; Felix de Quincy Marsh, 1906-1910; Albert Cuthbert Harrison, 1910-1921; William Harvard, 1922-1924; Jenkin Alban Davies, 1924-1932; William Featherstone, 1932-1944; John Selwyn Taborn, 1944-1961; Richard Sparkes, 1962-1969 (died in Wales, July 1997); Frank Giles, 1970-1981; William Smyth, 1983-1987 and David Ward, 1987-1993. Late arrival Mark Dearnley, commencing 1994, missed this montage by Eric Heather.

A thriving community spirit

Hook scouts

COMMUNITY spirit thrives in Hook even though the farming village of the past has long since been replaced by a busy neighbourhood with tens of thousands of motorists each day travelling up and down the Hook Road towards the A3 or M25.

The 1st Hook and 2nd Hook Scout groups are examples of this prevailing sense of community.

The 2nd Hook celebrated 25 years of scouting in 1988. It was founded by Surbiton policeman Reg Cooper in the icy January of 1963 and has grown to have a membership of around 200.

Originally, meetings were held at the former Hook Library, then a small hall at the rear of Hartfield Road, approached via a footpath next to the White Hart.

Mr Cooper then purchased a building contractors' hut in Hounslow for £500 and, piece by piece, transferred it to a new HQ behind Hook Parish Hall in 1971.

Some 5,000 boys received their scout training in 2nd Hook which has seen in excess of 100 leaders and assistants in its time.

Both the 1st and 2nd Hook have regular scout parades and band practices.

The 2nd Hook troop's disabled section was the first of its type when formed in 1965 and met with early resis-

A 1st Hook Scouts band parade in Hook Road c1976. On the left is the National Westminster bank, formerly Pointer's general stores, bakery, and post office in Hook's more rural times. Shopkeeper Mrs Lineham was particularly proud of the scouts and watched them from a balcony above Arcade Parade.

Hook vicar, Rev. Felix de Quincy Marsh, formed a Hook scout troop in 1909.

tance from the movement before it was recognised.

For the 1st Hook Scouts, the year 1998 is an important one in the group's history, for it marks its official diamond (75th) jubilee. The group was first registered in 1923 but it was, in fact, up and running as early as 1909.

The Edwardian troop was formed by the vicar of Hook from 1906 to 1910, Reverend Felix de Quincy Marsh, after the boy scout movement was launched nationally by Baden-Powell in 1908. It appears meetings were held at Hook School in Orchard Road. A leader just before the Great War was a Mr Barnes.

In 1923, a troop was officially registered and was run by Dickie Cole. A rover crew for older boys was established the following year.

The 1st Hook troop met in more recent times in a new building in Verona Drive which replaced the former prisoner of war Nissen hut relocated soon after 1948 from a POW site opposite the Lucky Rover public house, Hook Road.

Moor Lane after the great thunderstorm of Friday 6th July 1973. Rainfall was 4.65ins in two hours.

September 1997 was a sad time in Hook. after the Princess of Wales' death. The Cricketers mourned. and shops closed..

Coronation party, 1953

Residents of Bramham Gardens, Hook, were in party mood to celebrate the coronation of Queen Elizabth in June 1953.

Commemorating Enid Blyton

Gillian Baverstock, daughter of Enid Blyton, at Southernhay in 1997 with a copy of Enid's first book, Child Whispers, (1922).

Ex-Enid Blyton pupils Kathleen Sayer and John Thompson revisit Southernhay, Hook Road, in August 1997. Kathleen , sister of another pupil, Mollie, took piano lessons at the little school run by the young woman who became the world's most famous children's author.

About the author

MARK Davison lived in Hook for more than 20 years and as a child was taught at St Paul's School. His interest in writing started at the age of 11 when he brought out a school magazine called *Children's Monthly* in which the first prize for answering a quiz question correctly was a tube of Smarties. After secondary school in Kingston, he joined the *Kingston Borough News* and wrote several informative features on bygone Hook.

His newspaper career took him to Reigate where he became deputy editor of the *Surrey Mirror* in 1986. He has, with co-author Ian Currie, written a dozen other local history books including *Surrey In the Sixties*, *Surrey In the Seventies* and a county best-seller, the *Surrey Weather Book*, which has been reprinted five times. He now lives in Reigate but maintains close links with Hook though family and friends and has campaigned successfully over the years to keep Hook on the map and in the postal address.